Repetition, the Compulsion to Repeat, and the Death Drive

Dialog-on-Freud Series
Series Editor: M. Andrew Holowchak

The Dialog-on-Freud series invites authors to explore the history and practice of analytic therapies through critical analysis of and expatiation on the seminal work of Freud. It seeks books that critically scrutinize the numerous facets of Freud's work over the course of his life, that investigate how or to what extent Freud's thinking causally gave rise to the various sorts of therapies that currently exist, and that examine the relevance of Freud's thinking today for those therapies.

Titles in This Series

Freud's Theory of Culture: Eros, Loss, and Politics, by Abraham Drassinower
The Unconscious without Freud, by Rosemarie Spooner Sand
How Talking Cures: Revealing Freud's Contributions to All Psychotherapies, by Lee Jaffe
Freud's Theory of Dreams: A Philosophico-Scientific Perspective, by Michael T. Michael
Nabokov's Mimicry of Freud: Art as Science, by Teckyoung Kwon
How Culture Runs the Brain: A Freudian View of Collective Syndromes, by Jay Evans Harris
Repetition, the Compulsion to Repeat, and the Death Drive: An Examination of Freud's Doctrines, by M. Andrew Holowchak and Michael Lavin

Repetition, the Compulsion to Repeat, and the Death Drive

An Examination of Freud's Doctrines

M. Andrew Holowchak and Michael Lavin

LEXINGTON BOOKS
Lanham • Boulder • New York • London

Published by Lexington Books
An imprint of The Rowman & Littlefield Publishing Group, Inc.
4501 Forbes Boulevard, Suite 200, Lanham, Maryland 20706
www.rowman.com

Unit A, Whitacre Mews, 26-34 Stannary Street, London SE11 4AB

British Library Cataloguing in Publication Information Available

Library of Congress Cataloging-in-Publication Data

Library of Congress Cataloging-in-Publication Data Available
ISBN: 978-1-4985-7050-3 (cloth : alk. paper)
ISBN: 978-1-4985-6110-5 (electronic)

∞™ The paper used in this publication meets the minimum requirements of American National Standard for Information Sciences Permanence of Paper for Printed Library Materials, ANSI/NISO Z39.48-1992.

Printed in the United States of America

From ML:
for Roberta

Contents

Contents

Preface

This project began with a paper,[1] published in 2015, concerning the role of "repetition" in Freudian psychoanalysis. The motivation for the paper was the wholly ignored concept of repetition in the early stages of the development of Freud's views of psychoanalysis, both in its role as a therapeutic technique and as part of a theoretical system, and how such early uses of the term led to the compulsion to repeat and the death drive, each of which has been given much attention in the secondary literature.

In a 1922 encyclopedia article appropriately titled "Psycho-Analysis," Freud writes of "psychoanalysis" as "a procedure for investigating unconscious mental processes," "a method . . . for the treatment of neurotic disorders," and " a collection of psychological data . . . which is gradually being accumulated into a new scientific discipline"[2] (1922, *S.E.*, XVIII: 235). Consequently, psychoanalysis as a procedure for investigating unconscious mental processes is a depth psychology with metapsychological implications, a treatment for individual clients with neurotic disorders, or an analytic method and a comprehensive collection of psychological data as a new science. In this undertaking, we examine the role of repetition in all aspects of psychoanalysis—especially as it leads to an alteration of Freud's metapsychological thinking, pertaining to adoption of the death drive and motivated by his observations concerning the compulsion to repeat.

This book—a critical examination of Freud's uses of repetition as they lead to the compulsion to repeat and his infamous death drive—is in effect the first scholarly attempt to ground Freudian psychoanalysis on the concept of repetition. Like perhaps no other concept, repetition drove Freud to an understanding of human behavior through development of models of the human mind and a method of treating neurotic behavior.

Repetition, the Compulsion to Repeat, and the Death Drive: An Examination of Freud's Doctrines comprises three parts. Part I, "Some Early Uses of 'Repetition' in Psychoanalysis," examines repetition both in clinical therapy (chapter 1) and in Freud's use of phylogenetic explanation (chapter 2). Part II, composed of three chapters, outlines Freud's journey to his vaunted death drive. Chapter 3 concerns the road to *Beyond the Pleasure Principle.* The fourth chapter is an examination of *Beyond the Pleasure Principle*. Chapter 5 is an analysis of Freud's use of compulsion to repeat and the death drive post 1920. Last, part III is a critical analysis of Freud on repetition and the death drive. Why was Freud so wedded to his controversial death drive? That we answer in chapter 6. Chapter 7 concerns what can be salvaged from Freud's observations and speculations. Here readers will find that Holowchak, qua philosopher, and Lavin, qua clinician, have different answers when it comes to the death drive.

One of the key findings of this project is that "repetition" should be regarded as one of the axial concepts, perhaps *the* axial concept, of Freudian psychoanalysis, though it has never been awarded such a status. As creatures of habit, we are astonishingly repetitive—natural selection demands repetitive behaviors—and the nature and frequency of our repetitions, Freud came quickly to find, offered themselves as clues to our psychical normalcy, or abnormalcy. Through study of repetitions, he slowly developed a metapsychology of human functioning through adoption of concepts such as unconscious, repression, Oedipus complex, and libido, and developed theoretical models of the human mind such as the topographical model in 1900 and the structural model in 1923, with its full details in 1926. Through study of repetitions, he developed two of the bedrock concepts of psychoanalysis—compulsion to repeat and transference—the former leading to change of his model of drives by adding a death drive.

The book ends with a postscript that spells out a few of Lavin's concerns as a clinician and a jointly written essay, titled "A Reading of Freud's Epistemology: Realism or Perspectivism?"

NOTES

1. M. Andrew Holowchak and Michael Lavin, "Beyond the Death Drive: The Future of 'Repetition' and 'Repetition Compulsion' in Psychopathology," *Psychoanalytic Psychology*, vol. 32, no. 4, 645–68.
2. See also Freud's 1925 essay "Autobiographical Study" (1925, *S.E.*, XX: 70).

I

Some Early Uses of "Repetition" in Psychoanalysis

Chapter One

Repetition, Neuroses, and the General Theory of Neurosis

This chapter retraces Freud's ontogenetic uses of "repetition." We tell the ontogenetic story of the development of Freud's view of psychoanalysis as a theory and method for treating individuals with neurotic, borderline, and psychotic personality organization. Freud's treatment of his patients' complaints, combined with the study of his patient's and his own dreams, convinced him that both had unconscious determinants. He came to believe that the interpretation of dreams was a royal road to understanding the complaints of his patients. The creation of dreams and symptoms operated on the same principles. By understanding dreams, Freud came to believe he could understand his patients' symptoms as well. The mind relies on the same principles for constructing dreams as it does for symptoms. A trained therapist could interpret both dreams and symptoms. Repetition is a prominent factor in the formation of dreams and the formation of symptoms. Repetition saturates a life. Effective treatment often uses repetition.

Thus, to set the groundwork for Freud's use of "repetition" as it leads to "compulsion to repeat" and "the death drive"—topics of later chapters—we first tell the story of the development of Freud's views of psychoanalysis as clinical therapy, of how clinical insights buttressed perhaps the most influential theory of the human mind the world has ever seen, and of how Freud drew from other sciences, some now dated, to confirm his psychological insights.

We begin with repetition in psychoanalytic therapy.

REPETITION IN PSYCHOANALYTIC THERAPY

Polar Tugs

In October, 1885, Freud left for Paris to study for some six months under Jean-Martin Charcot at the Salpêtrière asylum, where hysteria was for the first time being scientifically studied by the celebrated neurologist Charcot. Charcot was experimenting with hypnosis, a method generally abjured by medical men (1888, *S.E.*, I: 76), as a tool for a heightened understanding of hysteria. Freud attended Charcot's lectures and demonstrations. What he learned astonished him. Charcot convinced him, first, that hysteria was a genuine—that is, conformable-to-laws—disorder.[1] Second, hysteria—which was rooted in the Greek word *hystera*, meaning "womb"—was not merely endemic to women. Third, Charcot's studies indicated that hysteria, resulting from "excitability in the different parts of the nervous system" and not alterations of the nervous system, seemed to be indifferent to anatomy—irreducible to any aberrant bodily condition, that is, a functional disorder. Fourth, Charcot demonstrated that hysterical symptoms were often brought about by trauma. Finally, Charcot was able to reproduce or repeat hysterical symptoms through use of hypnosis (1888, *S.E.*, I: 41, and 1925, *S.E.*, XX: 13).

Charcot's view of hypnosis Freud called somatic, as it was a physiologically altered condition of the nervous system brought about by external stimuli that influenced the body. There was, however, a necessary condition for a person to be hypnotizable. "The mechanism of some . . . of the manifestations of hypnotism is based upon physiological changes—that is, upon displacements of excitability in the nervous system, occurring without the participation of those parts of it which operate with consciousness." Hysteria was believed to be trauma-induced. That trauma, then, brought about a hypnotic state, which was found to be accessible by hypnosis.

What was Charcot's proposed method of therapy? Hypnosis, as a tool for access to the physiological substructure of hysteria, was of no therapeutic use. Yet under hypnosis, a therapist would use suggestion to counter the hysterical symptoms. Freud claimed, "Only neuropaths (especially hysterics) are hypnotizable" (1888, *S.E.*, I: 77–78).

Though influenced by Charcot, Freud was also attracted to the rival thesis of Ambrose-August Liébeault and Hippolyte Bernheim at Nancy. Liébeault and Bernheim maintained simply that hypnosis was not a signal of a degenerative neurological state, but merely a matter of suggestion (*Transfert*). "All the phenomena of hypnotism have the same origin: they arise, that is, from a suggestion, a conscious idea, which has been introduced into the brain of the hypnotized person by an external influence and has been accepted by him as though it had arisen spontaneously" (1888, *S.E.*, I: 77). Though thought to be a matter of suggestion, Liébeault and Bernheim used hypnosis qua suggestion to alleviate hysterical symptoms, which were themselves believed to be caused by a state of heightened suggestibility, similar to sleep. The two therapists developed a form of therapy, based on suggestion.[2] They were not always successful with their method, and, when they were successful, favorable results were not always long-lived.

Those two rival but antipodal explanations—somatic-based versus psychic-based—would prove to be polar tugs that enticed and haunted Freud throughout his career. Though convinced proper scientific explanation needed to be based on physiology, one of Freud's great contributions to science would be to show one could give scientifically legitimate explanations of human motivations and behavior without recourse to human physiology—that psychology had its own claim to be considered a science.

Freud waffled on the issue of hypnosis. Prior to seeing Bernheim in the summer of 1889, he loved Charcot's view.[3] The visit to Nancy inclined him to believe that hypnosis is suggestion, but the purchase was never complete. As late as 1921, he rejected hypnosis as suggestion in favor of the "naïf earlier one" (1921, *S.E.*, XVIII: 128, fn. 1). Freud may have wanted to believe that hypnosis was mere suggestion, but he could not sever himself from the view that there was some physiological link between hypnosis and hysteria—hence, the lure throughout his life of neurological metapsychological explanations as early as his unpublished *Project for a Scientific Psychology* (1895) and throughout Freud's life.

Freud learned plenty from his trip to France—enough to pave the way for a science of the psyche. First, each of these rival schools examined the therapeutic benefits of hypnosis as a means of alleviating the symptoms of hysteria, when hypnosis was in discredit. Thus, Freud saw firsthand that scientific advance may come through rejecting received views and having the daring to travel an unconventional path—a sentiment reflected years later in a letter to friend and confidant Wilhelm Fleiss (June 30, 1896), himself a most unconventional physician: "You have taught me that a bit of truth lurks behind every popular lunacy."[4] Second, the almost theatrical impressions of these two rival schools must have been lasting on the young neuroscientist. They bolstered the notion, already implanted in him by Brentano,[5] that physical effects could be psychologically induced. Freud wrote, as he reflected on the effect of his trip to France:

> With the idea of perfecting my hypnotic technique, I made a journey to Nancy in the summer of 1889 and spent several weeks there. I witnessed the moving spectacle of old Liébeault working among the poor women and children of the laboring classes. I was a spectator of Bernheim's astonishing experiments upon his hospital patients, and I received the profoundest impression of the possibility that there could be powerful mental processes which nevertheless remained hidden from the consciousness of men. (1925, *S.E.*, XX: 17)

Thus Freud's years in France proved life-changing. They set the stage for a psychology of the unconscious, psychoanalysis, to be fleshed out in major writings such as *The Interpretation of Dreams* and *The Ego and the Id* and significant metapsychological papers such as "The Unconscious," "Instincts and their Vicissitudes," and "Repression." Freud's psychoanalysis would be founded on an etiology of repression, methods of therapy, and a dated Lamarckian biology, each making significant use of repetition.

CATHARTIC THERAPY

Freud's first theory of neurosis—the cathartic model—was developed through his collaborative work, *Studies on Hysteria* (1895), with his older friend and mentor, the physician Josef Breuer.

In 1880, five years before Freud studied with Charcot, Breuer took on, as a favor to her family, a young, female patient, Bertha Pappenheim, whom they would make famous as "Anna O." Anna suffered from a variety of hysterical symptoms and Breuer found, quite by accident, a new method of symptom remediation. Upon hearing of the case, Freud pressed Breuer for details.

Anna's hysteria started when she began to nurse her sick father. She suffered from multiple symptoms through four phases of illness: a latent incubation (about six months, beginning July 1880), manifest illness (peculiar psychosis, convergent squinting, severe visual disturbances, paralyzing contractures, complete or partial paralysis of certain parts of her body, and reduced muscular contracture of right extremities; about four months), a period of somnambulism (about eight months), and a gradual winding down of mental states and symptoms (in June, 1882) (1895, *S.E.*, II: 21–22). What was most perplexing, Breuer discovered, was that Anna's symptoms began to disappear when she, under hypnosis or, more cautiously, at Breuer's suggestion, told stories to Breuer. Success in being able to recount the hallucinations of the day through hypnosis enabled her to wake up lucid and serene, calm enough for her to work in an efficient manner the next day. Breuer added, "If for any reason she was unable to tell me the story during her evening hypnosis, she failed to calm down afterwards, and on the following day she had to tell me *two* stories in order for this to happen." That suggested a mounting of inner tension of some sort, and with it, an increase of resistance. Anna herself dubbed this method the "talking cure" and, somewhat humorously, "chimney sweeping"[6] (1895, *S.E.*, II: 29–30).

Freud believed Breuer's method was a means of signal discovery, which would be the basis of psychoanalysis. He convinced a reticent Breuer to collaborate on and publish their findings, supported by case material. The result was the *Studies on Hysteria*—the beginning of psychoanalysis.

Certain pathological phenomena, wrote Freud, have traumatic, precipitating events that are psychical, not physical. In cases of traumatic neuroses, he added, a patient cannot see the causal link, as "the operative cause of the illness is not the trifling physical injury but the affect of fright—the psychical trauma" (1895, *S.E.*, II: 5–6). As an example of how such a pathological phenomenon can be removed, Freud offered the analogy of a virus. "The causal relation between the determining psychical trauma and the hysterical phenomenon is not of a kind implying that the trauma merely acts like an *agent provocateur* in releasing the symptom, which thereafter leads an independent existence." Thus, the memory of the psychical trauma "acts like a foreign body which long after its entry must continue to be regarded as an agent that is still at work." Hysterical symptoms—Anna O., for instance, had hydrophobia, which vanished when she related to Breuer a story concerning a friend's dog drinking water from an elegant bowl—are effects of that memory. Breuer and Freud said: "Each individual hysterical symptom immediately and permanently disappeared when we had succeeded in bringing clearly to light the memory of the event by which it was provoked and in arousing its accompanying affect, and when the patient had described that event in the greatest possible detail and had put the affect into words" (1895, *S.E.*, II: 6).

The key hypothesis, Freud noted, is that wakening the memory of the precipitating event with complete clarity is sufficient for removal of the symptom, provided the accompanying affect is aroused along with it. His insistence on the presence of an accompanying affect is an insistence on what is called abreaction. The hypothesis is that accurate recall of a pathogenic event for a symptom plus the relevant abreaction is sufficient for the symptom's removal. How is that possible? From his studies in France, Freud learned both that forgotten pathogenic memories were never lost, but capable of retrieval, and that there was a resisting force at work that kept them from being recalled. Freud stated the hypothesis as, "*Hysterics suffer mainly from reminiscences*" (1895, *S.E.*, II: 7).

How, on this etiological hypothesis, did treatment successes with hysterics occur? Breuer wrote "These findings—that in the case of this patient the hysterical phenomena disappeared as soon as the event which had given rise to them was reproduced in her hypnosis—made it possible to arrive at a therapeutic technical procedure which left nothing to be desired in its logical consistency and systematic application." Symptoms, then, were covert repetitions of actual traumata, and as such, each symptom offered clues to unveiling the actual psychogenic trauma. When one through hypnosis or, more cautiously, suggestion went back to the occasion which triggered the symptom, the symptom would disappear, if the patient experienced the associated abreaction with the memory (1895, *S.E.*, II: 35).

In short, through hypnosis, the first instant of reproduction of an event causing a symptom with abreaction is sufficient for removal of that symptom. Each symptom is to be treated independently of all others, and treatment of a symptom consists of "narrating" or retracing each occurrence of a symptom in reverse order—from latest appearance to earliest appearance. Last, efficient use of the method should result in permanent removal of the symptom. Thus the method of catharsis is itself a repetition. The ultimate therapeutic moment is a repetition or reexperience of a traumatic event with its associated emotion.

The method is "cathartic" because some sort of dammed-up emotional energy, unable to find discharge, is converted into symptoms. A hysterical person's physical symptoms are conversions of dammed-up affect. Therapy consists in removing the symptoms to free the emotional energy for uses other than disguised repetition of the traumatic event. It is an early example of displacement; the emotion is transferred to the symptom without the actual trauma being experienced. The fear of drinking from a dog-contaminated bowl, a bowl also used by the patient, becomes a fear of drinking, while the repellant thought that she is sharing a water bowl with a dog has no conscious occurrence—that is, is repressed.

Freud, with a preference for cure with an explanation over symptom removal without etiological understanding, also attempted to give a dynamical explanation that included a primitive, inchoate topography. He noted that mnemonic elements of pathogenic events have three forms—linear-chronological, concentric-pathogenic, and branching-dynamic—and expatiated on each.

First, mnemonic elements display a linear, chronological arrangement. "These files . . . make the work of analysis more difficult by the peculiarity that, in reproducing the memories, they reverse the order in which these originated. The freshest and newest experience in the file appears first, as an outer cover, and last of all comes the experience with which the series in fact began" (1895, *S.E.*, II: 288).

Second, mnemonic elements have a concentric stratification around the pathogenic nucleus, in a manner that is proportional to the resistances an analyst faces. "The contents of each particular stratum are characterized by an equal degree of resistance, and that degree increases in proportion as the strata are neared to the nucleus." Those strata, as layers, are accessible to consciousness in proportion to their remoteness from the core. "The most peripheral strata contain the memories (or files), which, belonging to different themes, are easily remembered and have always been clearly conscious." The deeper one goes, the harder for patients to get at the relevant memories. "Near the nucleus we come upon memories which the patient disavows even in reproducing them" (1895, *S.E.*, II: 289).

Finally, mnemonic elements form a logical and dynamic branching arrangement of converging lines "according to thought-content." He elaborated. The chain is comparable to "the zig-zag line in the solution of a Knight's Move problem [in the game of chess], which cuts across the squares in the diagram of the chess-board." Then there is a "ramifying system of lines and more particularly to a converging one." Threads meet at nodal points and then become one. In these passages are early expressions of Freud's hypothesis of over determination. He concluded, "It is very remarkable how often a symptom is determined in several ways, is 'overdetermined'" (1895, *S.E.*, II: 289–90). The symptom is not only produced, it is overproduced, hence, repetition of a symptom can follow multiple paths.

The linear, concentric, and branching patterns used by Freud can clarify some of the difficulties in applying the cathartic method as a treatment for hysteria. These difficulties include complexity of symptom-formation, over-representation in the symptom (a form of repetition), and resistance, also a repetitive phenomenon that occurs due to lack of access to consciousness. This is not to mention the large number of traumata that an ordinary case of hysteria, for example Anna O.'s large list of independent symptoms, requires on the cathartic account.

Perhaps the largest difficulty was that the cathartic method, ignoring the conventional medical dictum to treat causes, not symptoms, was symptomatic, not causal, As a symptomatic method, it "does not influence the basic causes of hysteria and is therefore unable to prevent new symptoms developing in the place of those that have been removed" (1895, *S.E.*, II: 262–64).

This limitation is surprising given Freud's comparison of a trauma to a virus. Removal of each trauma or virus would seem to be a causal account of cure. Each symptom is independent, but on the face of it that is hard to believe. Hysteria, as Freud and Breuer knew, had typical clinical presentations. This similarity across cases favors the idea of a common underlying pathology for hysteria. A satisfactory account of hysteria, at least from a medical perspective, should be more than an enumeration of symptoms and the traumata, presumably different for each patient, that generate the symptoms.

This limitation in Freud's early hypotheses about hysteria would eventually force Freud to a nuanced, deeper view of pathogenic explanation, which would ultimately entail a fuller and historically richer account of hysteria, such that a trained therapist would have access to the underlying causal process, and which would prompt Freud to explanatory hypotheses derived from the topography of the human mind that his work on dreams was leading him to accept, with mind's typography being an inference to the best explanation from Freud's discovery of the interpretability of dreams.

The need for a more nuanced view initially was Freud's belief, based on his own clinical observations, that the pathogens of hysteria were sexual.

Here he parted company with Breuer, who was all along, at best, a disobliging participant in their collaborative efforts.[7] In short, while Breuer, who spoke only of Anna O.'s underdeveloped sexuality in his case study (1895, *S.E.*, II: 21), did not see sexuality as a factor in Anna's hysteria, Freud saw a sexual pathogen in each of the four cases he analyzed in the *Studies on Hysteria* and presumed different sexual factors to result in different sorts of neurosis. "In the first place I was obliged to recognize that, in so far as one can speak of determining causes which lead to the *acquisition* of neuroses, their aetiology is to be looked for in *sexual* factors. There followed the discovery that different sexual factors, in the most general sense, produce different pictures of neurotic disorders" (1895, *S.E.*, II: 257). In time, Freud traced these sexual factors to different sexual developmental histories in *Three Essays on Sexuality* (1905, *S.E.*, VII: 123–245).

THE SEDUCTION HYPOTHESIS

Freud's conjecture of a connection between sexuality and neuroses led to a next step. Freud posited that the link between pathogen and symptom was sexual and an actual physical event in the hysterical patient's biography. As early as November 27, 1893, he wrote to Wilhelm Fleiss: "Altogether I have hit upon the idea to tie anxiety not to a psychic but rather to a *physical* consequence of sexual abuse. I was led to this by a wonderfully pure case of anxiety neurosis following *coitus interruptus* in a totally placid and totally frigid woman. Otherwise it does not make any sense."[8] Freud was moving toward his seduction hypothesis.

Three years later, in "Aetiology of Hysteria" (1896), Freud embraced the seduction hypothesis. Childhood seduction, often in the form of molestation by a parent or close relative, is asserted as a necessary condition for neurosis—a shift from the Freud-Breuer hypothesis regarding symptoms from a wide variety of traumata. This early hypothesis was symptom-oriented, and therapy continued until symptoms ceased as a result of an affective reexperience or repetition of the initial trauma. Subsequent clinical experience based on the initial hypothesis was disappointing. Clinical work showed symptoms often returned, or new ones surfaced and so the method did not cure. By the time of "Aetiology of Hysteria," he wrote, "The symptoms of hysteria (apart from the stigmata) are determined by certain experiences of the patient's which have operated in a traumatic fashion and which are being reproduced in his psychical life in the form of mnemonic symbols" (1896, *S.E.*, II: 192–93). Therapy—aiming at getting at the underlying causes of the sexual symptoms, thereby seemed to offer, if Freud's conjectures about the role of sexual trauma in hysteria were correct, promise of complete cure is now etiological. Sexual abuse causes hysteria in persons.

There are two principles that guided Freud's etiological speculations concerning a trauma creation of a repetitive symptom: suitability and strength. First, a suspected pathogen must be relevantly suitable as a causal determinant of a hysterical symptom. Second, a suspected pathogen must have sufficient traumatic force to bring about a hysterical symptom (1896, *S.E.*, II: 194). Freud then said that if the memory, uncovered in therapy, fails to answer to the two conditions, "perhaps behind the first traumatic scene there may be concealed the memory of a second, which satisfies our requirements better and whose reproduction has a greater therapeutic effect." That means that the first scene is relevant only insofar as it serves as "a connecting link in the chain of association." He then added, "Perhaps this situation may repeat itself; inoperative scenes may be interpolated more than once, as necessary transitions in the process of reproduction, until we finally make our way from the hysterical symptom to the scene which is really operative traumatically and which is satisfactory in every respect, both therapeutically and analytically" (1986, *S.E.*, II: 195).

To the principles of sufficient relevance and force, Freud superadded several others. There are the mnemonic principle: "No hysterical symptom can arise from a real experience alone, but that in every case the memory of earlier experiences awakened in association to it plays a part in causing the symptom" (1896, *S.E.*, II: 197); the principle of sexual etiology: "Whatever case and whatever symptom we take as our point of departure, in the end we infallibly come to the field of sexual experience" (1896, *S.E.*, II: 199); the principle of unconscious etiology: "Hysterical symptoms are derivatives of memories which are operating unconsciously" (1896, *S.E.*, II: 211–12); the principle of childhood etiology: "Infantile sexual experiences are the fundamental precondition for hysteria, are, as it were, the disposition for it and that it is they which create the hysterical symptoms, but that they do not do so immediately, but remain without effect to begin with and only exercise a pathogenic action later, when they have been aroused after puberty in the form of unconscious memories" (1896, *S.E.*, II: 212); and of course the principle of overdetermination: "Hysterical symptoms are overdetermined" (1896, *S.E.*, II: 216).

Freud glossed the analytic attitude at this point in his career thus, "At bottom of every case of hysteria there are *one or more occurrences of premature sexual experience*, occurrences which belong to the earliest years of childhood but which can be reproduced through the work of psycho-analysis in spite of the intervening decade" (1896, *S.E.*, II: 203). Consequently, symptoms are on analysis revealed to be repetitions of that premature sexual experience. Freud arrived at what is commonly called his Seduction Theory: Early childhood seduction is a necessary causal condition for neurosis.

Wish-Fulfillment Hypothesis

After abandoning his Seduction Theory, grounded on eighteen cases of "observed" sexual etiologies and eighteen avowed successful treatments (1896, *S.E.*, II: 199), infantile sexuality came to the fore and the large number of reported sex-abuse cases now was taken principally as youthful wish-fantasies of patients, following his wish-fulfillment thesis in *Interpretation of Dreams*.[9] In his case study *Dora* in 1905, Freud wrote of discovering a rule, "which I had found confirmed over and over again by experience," that "a symptom signifies the representation—the realization—of a phantasy with a sexual content, that is to say, it signifies a sexual situation." In short, "one of the meanings of a symptom is the representation of a sexual phantasy"—that is, fulfillment through repetition (1905, *S.E.*, VII: 46–47). Sexual scenes in patients' dreams reinforced sexual wish-fantasy. Thus it was natural for Freud to follow his work on dreams with a work on sexuality that focused on infantile sexuality.

That work was *Three Essays on the Theory of Sexuality* (1905–1925), considered by many, even Freud, to be his *magnum opus* next to *Interpretation of Dreams.*[10] The work began humbly—an opuscule of some eighty pages. By the sixth edition, published in 1925, the humble booklet was expanded 50 percent. It is curious that no apparent attempt was made to update it to accommodate theoretical shifts that had occurred during that twenty-year period. It, as well as the true magnum opus, remained a work relying on the Topographic Model of the psychical apparatus.

This work of sexual development has three parts—sexual aberrations, infantile sexuality, and transformations of puberty.

Freud began with sexual aberrations such as inversion (homosexuality) and bisexuality. Inversion, he stated, is neither a degenerative human condition nor is it purely, if at all, innate.[11] Following Krafft-Ebing, he added that every person has masculine and feminine brain centers that are under the guidance of the sex gland at puberty. Prior to puberty, individuals are entirely at the mercy of a sexual drive (*Trieb*[12]), to be understood for the moment as "a measure of the demand made upon the mind for work"—independent of the sex gland. He concluded that abnormal cases show that sexual drive and sexual object are contingently "soldered together" and that the sexual drive is "in the first instance independent of its object" and not due to its object's inherent attractions (1905, *S.E.*, VII: 136–48). True deviations, perversions, are activities that go beyond the sexual regions of the body—genitals, mouth, and anus—and linger over substitutive regions (1905, *S.E.*, VII: 149–60). From such observations, Freud concluded that resistance is at play to restrain the sexual drive and that the sexual drive itself is not simple, but complex (1905, *S.E.*, VII: 162).

Freud then turned to "Infantile Sexuality," a topic he thought crucial for grasping the various neuroses, since he never renounced an implausible and subsequently elaborated hypothesis that neurosis was a disturbance in the normal development of infantile sexual development and that neurotic symptoms were repetitions that offered clues to that disturbance. Memories of the formative years of childhood lag behind other mental activities, though the impressions of those early events have "left the deepest traces on our minds and have had a determining effect upon the whole of our later development" (1905, *S.E.*, VII: 259–60). Development involves sexual diphasism as well as the Oedipus complex[13]—a critical point in the psychosexual stages of sexual development.[14]

We begin with the pregenital, autoerotic phase—comprising the oral, anal, and phallic stages.

The oral, cannibalistic stage is roughly from birth to one and one-half years of age. Infants derive nourishment as well as great pleasure from suckling at a mother's breast. Over time, the lips become an erotogenic zone through taking in warm milk and sucking by itself, as a hedonic repetition, becomes a substitutive source of erotic satisfaction through association. "The need for repeating the sexual satisfaction now becomes detached from the need for taking nourishment—a separation which becomes inevitable when the teeth appear and food is no longer taken in only by sucking, but is also chewed up" (1905, *S.E.*, VII: 181–82).

From one and one-half to three years of age, there is the anal, sadistic stage. Here there is "the opposition between two [antipodal] currents . . . that runs through all sexual life." Activity is the need for mastery through somatic musculature; passivity is the need for mastery through the erotogenic mucous membrane of the anus. Erotogenic stimulation here consists of use of violent muscular contractions to hold back stool to produce painful and pleasurable sensations (1905, *S.E.*, VII: 185–87). Because of the pleasure found in holding back the stool—that is, having a sense of control—and the eventual pleasure of its release, heightened because of its delay, the experience is repeated.[15] Here the child learns control of pleasure and pain through control of anal tension. This stage provides the base for ambivalence.

Third, there is the phallic, oedipal stage (roughly, from three to five or six years). As the boy's first object is his mother's breast, the mother, by caring for her child's bodily needs, becomes his first seducer. However long the child has been weaned, that has been too little and too short. He continually wishes for more. No seduction is complete without constant repetition. The boy sees himself as his mother's lover, the rival of his father. He eventually shows his organ to her, but it is undersized in comparison with his father's, and so he envies, and execrates, his father.[16] When his mother becomes aware of the rivalry, she forbids the boy's repetitive handling of his organ.

The boy is threatened with castration by the father. The threat, the most anxiety-laden episode of his entire life, leads to a period of sexual latency.

To preserve his organ, the boy becomes sexually passive, feminine. He renounces his mother and his own masculinity and becomes insouciant toward his father. He gives up masturbation, and enters into a period of latency. He identifies with his father through sublimation and takes on his father's moral scheme as his own. That results in the formation of the boy's sense of conscience (later, superego, though the superego is not part of the Three Essays conceptual scheme) and the repression of his former lust for his mother. Freud wrote, "One of the clearest indications that a child will later become neurotic is to be seen in an insatiable demand for his parents' affection" (1905, *S.E.*, VII: 194–97, 223).

We come here to the second phase, comprising only the hetero-erotic genital stage, from puberty to adulthood. Genital mastery comes in proper substitutive satisfaction—that is, sublimation. "A good portion of the symptomatology of the neuroses which I have traced to disturbances of the sexual processes," Freud wrote, "is expressed in disturbances of other, non-sexual, somatic functions; and this circumstance, which has hitherto been unintelligible, becomes less puzzling if it is only the counterpart of the influences which bring about the production of sexual excitation" (1905, *S.E.*, VII: 206).

So we arrive at Freud's libido theory—a 1915 addition to the third part of the book. "Libido" he defined as "a quantitatively variable force which could serve as a measure of processes and transformations occurring in the field of sexual excitation." It is to be distinguished from the energy that underlies other forms of psychical activity, though libido is not derived from the sexual parts of the body only. "Ego-libido" he called the mental representation of that quantity of libido, whose production, increase or diminution, and distribution or displacement enables the psychotherapist to explain psychosexual phenomena. Ego-libido is, thus, the "great reservoir" from which object-attachments are formed. "The narcissistic libidinal cathexis of the ego is the original state of things, realized in earliest childhood, and is merely covered by the later extrusions of libido, but in essentials persists behind them. When one develops object-attachments, ego-libido is cathected to objects—i.e., it becomes object-libido" (1905, *S.E.*, VII: 217–18). The motivation for libido theory here is likely Darwinian: Animal behavior simply betrays fundamentally self-preservative and erotic behaviors.

In summary, neuroses occur in this line of Freud's thought because of developmental disturbances. Neuroses have roots in the normal development of early sexual life. Symptoms, understood aright as repetitions, are recurrent manifestations of a recurrent unconscious wish or impulse—to return to that time when sexual impulses readily found expression. Symptoms, hence, are viewed as wish-driven repetitions.

REPETITION AND THE ONTOGENY OF NEUROSIS

Symptoms are, on Freud's sexual theory of etiology, meaning-laden repetitions—clues to the trained psychoanalyst to, among other things, the patient's underlying sexual developmental history. In each type of neurosis, there is fixation to a "particular phase in the past," and it is an analyst's job to disclose that sexual fixation, hence the possibility of a science or general theory of neurosis. Overall, fixation to a phase of the past is by far more common than neurosis, as not every fixation is sufficiently strong and suitable for neurosis. "Every neurosis includes a fixation of that kind, but not every fixation leads to a neurosis, coincides with a neurosis, or arises owing to a neurosis" (1917, *S.E.*, XVI: 276). The idea that predisposing factors do not have disease as an inevitable outcome is a commonplace in medicine. Even identical twins are not perfectly concordant for schizophrenia.

"Neurotic symptoms have a sense, like parapraxes and dreams [see chapter 2], and . . . they have an intimate connection with the patient's experiences." An analyst's task then is "to discover, in respect to a senseless idea and a pointless action, the past situation in which the idea was justified and the action served a purpose" (1917, *S.E.*, XVI: 334). Here we illustrate through obsessional neurosis, anxiety hysteria, and traumatic neurosis.[17]

In "The Disposition to Obsessional Neurosis" (1913), Freud said that pathogenic determinants to neurosis are constitutional and accidental—in more familiar terms, due to nature and nurture. The science of his day worked on assumption of a constitutional determinant. Such a constitutional determinant allows for a clinging to a prior stage—a "point of fixation." An external disturbance might lead to regression, a return to a fixation point, but disposition to fixation is, added Freud, biological, and psychoanalysis has nothing to add (1913, *S.E.*, XII: 317–18)—or so it seems.

Freud did mention a tack taken in an earlier work, "Two Principles on Mental Functioning" (1911). "The order in which the main forms of psychoneuroses are usually enumerated—Hysteria, Obsessional Neurosis, Paranoia, Dementia Praecox—corresponds (even though not quite exactly) to the order of the ages at which the onset of these disorders occurs." Hysteria is observable in earliest childhood; obsessional neurosis, in the second, genital phase; and the other two, after puberty. The last two, the last to appear in sexual development, have features that are resistant to psychoanalytic treatment: megalomania, withdrawal from reality, and resistance to the development of transference. Such difficulties suggest that their dispositional fixation must be prior to object-choice—in the earliest, autoerotic and narcissistic phase of childhood. If so, then the dispositional fixation of the two transference neuroses—hysteria and obsessional neurosis—which are observable in early childhood, are in the later phases of libidinal development (1913, *S.E.*, XII: 318–19).

Freud then offered the example of a female patient, suffering for several years from anxiety hysteria. Her anxiety hysteria changed so that her presentation became that of an obsessional neurosis, in contradiction to the biological thesis, assuming the initial diagnosis was not mistaken. Freud insisted on his initial diagnosis of hysteria. "The obsessional neurosis was not a further reaction to the same trauma which had first provoked the anxiety hysteria; it was a reaction to the second experience, which had completely wiped out the first." The woman developed anxiety hysteria, fantasies of seduction by her husband in the hopes of having a child, upon learning she could not have children by her husband. Her husband grasped her anxiety, and for the first time, failed in sexual intercourse, and took a trip. The woman, believing her husband now to be impotent, reacted with a compulsion for "scrupulous washing and cleanliness and extremely energetic protective measures" against injuries others might fear she could do to them. Those were "reaction-formations against her own *anal-erotic* and *sadistic* impulses." Hence Freud's inclination was to posit a pre-genital stage with anal-erotic and sadistic impulses (1913, *S.E.*, XII: 320–21), with symptoms triggered by post-adolescent events; perhaps "the choice of an object under the influence of the ego-instincts, at a time at which the sexual instincts had not yet assumed their final shape." What is left is a "fixation at the stage of the pregenital sexual organization" (1913, *S.E.*, XII: 325). All such regressions, of course, are repetitions, as they repeat in the present a form of fixation in the patient's past.

Repetition, as a key feature of neurotic behavior, is not so astonishing once one realizes that libidinal attachments are difficult to reconfigure. Also repetition is a standard element of normal sexual behavior. As one scholar notes, "In thumb-sucking 'the need for repeating the sexual satisfaction now becomes detached from the need to take in nourishment,' and becomes an independent sexual aim, with a second erotogenic zone (besides the lips) being created by the child, a part of his own body, the reason for the activity being called 'auto-erotic.'"[18] Similarly, the actions in erotogenic zones are repetitions. The difference is that in neurotic symptoms, there is that element of compulsiveness.

ANXIETY HYSTERIA

As we saw in chapter 1, part of Freud's earliest work in France was the study of hysteria under Charcot. Hysteria was a neurosis. Charcot and his followers, as well as Bernheim of the Nancy School, were pioneers in making the study of hysteria a scientific enterprise. Prior to becoming an object of scientific study, hysterics had been ridiculed, exorcised, and even burned (1888, *S.E.*, I: 41).

Treatment for anxiety hysteria is complicated by nature of the disorder. There are three possible targets for interventions: the hysterical disposition, the hysterical outbreaks, and individual hysterical symptoms. In Freud's view, the hysterical disposition cannot be eradicated, and the best method is prophylaxis—avoidance of overstressing the nervous system. Hysterical outbreaks are more difficult still and, even with intervention, "successes are rare." Patients need to be removed from their regular routine—especially the circumstances in which the outbreak first occurred. Complete isolation at a sanitarium is often the best method, as it involves "*traitement moral*" and allows for nutritional improvement. Last, treatment of individual hysterical symptoms cannot occur unless hysterical outbreaks are no longer occurring. During active hysterical outbreaks, a symptom, if removed, returns—that is, its successful removal is a Pyrrhic victory. Therapeutic effort is squandered as the conquered symptom is replaced by a new symptom. Drugs are also ill advised. Other alternative treatments included open-air living, hydrotherapy, electrotherapy, and arsenic and iron medication to improve circulation. Still other treatment relied on the same strategy as treatment of the constitution factor did, the "removal of sources of [physical] stimulus" (1888, *S.E.*, I: 53–56).

In "Hysterical Phantasies and their Relation to Bisexuality" (1908), Freud spotted a link between hysterical attacks and daydreaming. "Every hysterical attack which I have been able to investigate up to the present has proved to be an involuntary irruption of day-dreams of this kind." Why? Fantasies, once conscious, can become unconscious when the fantasizer gives them up, because of, say, newfound regard for moral approbation. Once unconscious, they can become pathogenic and express themselves as symptoms and attacks. He recounts a patient who had burst into tears on the street. She imagined a relationship with a certain well-known pianist and that she had his child and that he had deserted her and their child and left them penniless (1908, *S.E.*, IX: 160).

Unconscious fantasies are alleged to be sexual. "It is identical with the phantasy which served to give him sexual satisfaction during a period of masturbation," so long as masturbation is grasped in its widest erotogenic sense. Here fantasy and self-gratification become fused. If a person gives up the act, the fantasy cannot be forgotten, but is relegated to the unconscious, because a genuine source of pleasure, once established via repetition, cannot be renounced without work. If the subject does not find a substitutive outlet for the libido through sublimation, then the fantasy will find an outlet as a pathological symptom. Thus "hysterical symptoms are nothing other than unconscious phantasies brought into view through 'conversion,'" which is a disguised repetition. Through expression of the hysterical symptom, "the giving up of the habit of masturbation is in fact undone," and that allows for a repetition—that is, "a restoration of the original, primary sexual satisfaction" is in some measure achieved (1908, *S.E.*, IX: 161–62).

In treating hysterics, at this stage of Freud's thinking, an analyst works from symptoms to the unconscious fantasies behind them—thereby making them conscious to a patient. The content of unconscious fantasies thus "corresponds completely to the situations in which satisfaction is consciously obtained by perverts" (1908, *S.E.*, IX: 162).

Freud made nine claims about hysterical symptoms. They are (1) mnemonic symbols of operative traumatic representations, (2) substitutes that are produced by conversion "for the associative return of these traumatic experiences," (3) expressions of wish fulfillment, (4) expressions that function to fulfill the wish, (5) symbols of sexual satisfactions, (6) symbols that correspond to a return of an archaic mode of sexual satisfaction, a mode real in infancy and that has been repressed, (7) symbols that arise as compromise formations of an unconscious impulse seeking sexual satisfaction and an censor impulse seeking to repress that satisfaction, (8) expressions that sometimes take control of nonsexual unconscious impulses, and (9) symbols that are essentially bisexual. Claims 2 and 6 show plainly that repetition is fundamental to formation of symptoms (1908, *S.E.*, IX: 163–65).

Three cautionary points here are in order. First, its textual basis rests on writing that pre-dated Freud's structural model of id, ego, and superego. Second, its textual basis also precedes Freud's dual-drive theory. Third, its textual basis also precedes Freud's ground-breaking 1926 comprehension of signal identify and its role in psychopathology.

Freud also discussed hysteria, here "anxiety hysteria," years later in lecture 25 of his *Introductory Lectures on Psycho-Analysis*—"Anxiety." All people are biologically structured so that they react to danger. In that, they have anxiety rooted in an external threat, such as a soldier's fear during a bombardment. When a person substitutes a symptom for the anxiety that a situation should have elicited, that is anxiety hysteria. "In neurotic anxiety the ego is making a similar attempt at flight from the demand by its libido, that it is treating this internal danger as though it were an external one." Neurotic anxiety "is put to an abnormal employment" (1917, *S.E.*, XVI: 404–5)—the result being phobia. "Patients who suffer from agoraphobia," for instance, "often repeat the same features in their symptoms with wearisome monotony: they are afraid of enclosed spaces, of large open squares, of lengthy roads and streets" (1917, *S.E.*, XVI: 270). This account is at odds with a signal-anxiety account. On it, the anxiety is not a substitute for a representation of an event. Instead it is an alarm bell, a warning that an unconscious but superego-intolerable wish or impulse is threatening to become conscious. The anxiety triggers defenses (rigid and repetitive in cases of neuroses) to stop the emergence of the intolerable wish or impulse that makes repetitive efforts to attain entry into consciousness. If the repetitions are frequent, the result is chronic anxiety as well as chronic repetitions of ineffective efforts to bring it to an end. This account of the role, causes, and consequences of anxiety has no equivalent in the period under discussion.

OBSESSIONAL NEUROSIS

The psychiatry of his day, asserted Freud again in *Introductory Lectures on Psycho-Analysis*, has done nothing with obsessional neurosis other than giving "names to the different obsessions" and categorizing those with the neurosis as "dégénérés supérieurs." Yet psychoanalysis has shown "it is possible to get permanently rid of these strange obsessional symptoms" (1917, *S.E.*, XVI: 260–61).

Freud supported his claim of permanent removal of obsessional symptoms with the case of a woman, some thirty years of age, to whom we refer in the introduction of this section on ontogeny of neuroses. The woman would, several times each day, rush from her room to an adjoining room, take a position near a table in the middle of the room, ring for her housemaid, and then dismiss her with an arbitrary errand or without one. She had married a man much her senior ten years ago, and her husband proved impotent on their wedding day. He rushed out of the bedroom, after each failed attempt at lovemaking, and again rushed later in to try unsuccessfully once more. Concerned about what her housemaid might say about a clean bedsheet—she was a virgin—the disappointed bride poured red ink on the sheet. Freud labored over the connection between the wedding night and her obsessional behavior until the woman one day showed Freud the table she frequented in the adjoining room. Its tablecloth too had a large red stain in it (1917, *S.E.*, XVI: 261–62).

The woman, in rushing several times each day to and from the table and ringing for her housemaid, was not only imitating her husband, but also vindicating him. And so, "the obsessional action . . . appears to have been a representation, a repetition, of the significant scene." Freud added, "We see . . . that she was not simply repeating the scene, she was continuing and at the same time correcting it; she was putting it right" (1917, *S.E.*, XVI: 262–623).

Consequently, in the case of obsessional neurotics, the tendency to repeat is at the heart of the neurosis. Those repetitions have a rhythm and such actions are "isolated from other actions"[19] (1917, *S.E.*, XVI: 269–70).

The great contribution of psychoanalysis to understanding the acts of obsessional neurotics is showing that their compulsions are pregnant with meaning, unconscious to them. Analysis shows that compulsions begin as defenses for agents—repressions of an obsession the symptoms of which act as compromise formations between "warring forces of the mind." Freud wrote, "As the illness progresses . . . actions which were originally mostly concerned with maintaining the defence come to approximate more and more to the proscribed actions through which the drive was able to find expression in childhood" (1907, *S.E.*, IX: 123–25).

Freud's most famous case of obsessional neurosis was that of Ernst Lanzer, the celebrated Rat Man. The case was characterized by obsessional fears, compulsive behaviors, and prohibitions—the ensemble a result of fear of his father's death and fear that something might happen to his lady friend and future wife. He entertained obsessive ideas such as a strong desire to cut his throat with a razor (1909, *S.E.*, X: 158), a need to lose weight, a passion to protect his lady friend, a compulsion for counting after flashes of lightning, and even an obsession for mere understanding (1909, *S.E.*, X: 188–90). The last obsession manifested itself in a compulsion to ask any discussant to repeat something just said—"What was it you said just then?"—which unsurprisingly made him a nuisance. Each request for a repetition of what had just been said was caused by his obsession with the meaningfulness of every syllable uttered. He worried that missing a syllable meant missing the meaning of what he was being told.

Freud mentioned another of Lanzer's compulsive acts he did again and again under the guise of protecting his girlfriend. He would remove a stone from a path that her carriage would travel, but later put back the stone, after obsessing that moving it was an error. Replacing the stone exhibited his ambivalence as well as a sense of Lanzer's consciously aiming to abate his obsession—that is, the secondary obsession of trying to undo his compulsive act. In Lanzer's case, obsessional neurosis differs from anxiety hysteria. In the latter, opposing impulses find simultaneous expression; in the former, opposing impulses find distinct expressions (1909, *S.E.*, X: 191–92).

A key event that triggered Lanzer's obsessional thoughts and compulsive actions, said Freud, was a story, told to him by a certain Czech captain he chanced to meet, about an ancient form of torture in China. The torturer strapped a large pot with live rats to his victim's buttocks. The rats, in time, would create a path of escape by gnawing through and beyond the victim's anus (1909, *S.E.*, X: 166).

Freud's treatment, lasting about one year, said Freud, "led to a complete restoration of the patient's personality, and to the removal of his inhibitions" (1909, *S.E.*, X: 155). That proved not to be the case.[20]

Traumatic Neurosis

In Freud's early work with Breuer on cathartic therapy, both worked on the assumption that hysterical symptoms were the result of some situation, sufficiently traumatic (1917, *S.E.*, XVI: 275). Hence therapy involved disclosure of that trauma to remove the symptom. Yet by 1900, Freud formally repudiated that method, as he came to realize that the reality of the "trauma" was a dead end for understanding neurosis. What mattered was a child's perception of some event, and that perception was wish-based. Thus he developed the wish-fulfillment model along with a depth-psychology etiology, founded on key polysemous concepts such as repression and the unconscious, which would have a long evolution in psychoanalytic speculation.

Traumatic neuroses would always prove problematic for Freud—"nor have we succeeded in bringing them into harmony with our views" (1917, *S.E.*, XVI: 274)—because they seemed to leave no room for childhood wishes, as they did on the cathartic theory.

In lecture 18 of his *Introductory Lectures on Psychoanalysis*, Freud turned to the issue of traumatic neuroses. "The traumatic neuroses give a clear indication that a fixation to the moment of the traumatic accident lies at their root. These patients regularly repeat the traumatic situation in their dreams; where hysteriform attacks occur that admit of an analysis, we find that the attack corresponds to a complete transplanting of the patient into the traumatic situation—as if a patient needs to complete something about the traumatic situation" (1917, *S.E.*, XVI: 274–75). Thus traumatic neuroses are characterized by fixation on the traumatic moment and repeated returns to that moment, especially in dreams, as if to work out or to complete something with a tolerable denouement.

Repetitions of the trauma point to the ineliminable "economic" factor in mental processes. The experience proves traumatic in that it occurs "within a short period of time," and "presents the mind with an increase of stimulation too powerful to be dealt with or worked off in the normal way"—thus, the possibility of "permanent disturbances." Yet existence of cases in which no "traumatic" cause of nosology can be found—for instance, a case of a girl's erotic fixation on her father, apparent passage of the fixation, and subsequent return in symptoms of obsessional neurosis—shows that "the formula [of a real early life trauma] is not sufficiently comprehensive" (1917, *S.E.*, XVI: 275), hence his abandonment of the cathartic method. Freud failed to amplify.

Freud revisited to the problem of traumatic neuroses in lecture 29 of his New Introductory Lectures on Psycho-Analysis. In it Freud discusses, inter alia, a revision to the theory of dreams, which posits that dreams are generated by and fulfillments of unconscious wishes (1900, *S.E.*, IV: 121–22). That revision is needed because of anxiety dreams—specifically, dreams of punishment. How can they be wish fulfillments?

There is, strictly speaking, no contravention of wish fulfillment if we grasp that the wish fulfilled is not unconscious, but that of "the critical, censoring and punishing agency of the mind"—here the superego, a concept unavailable to Freud at the time of *The Interpretation of Dreams*. Punishment in such dreams is in effect a corrective to the wish behind the dream (1932, *S.E.*, XXII: 27–28).

Yet two difficulties remain. First, consider "a severe psychical trauma." Consider for illustration a recurrent dream of a soldier, who repeatedly finds himself back at the front and reliving horrific moments. What sort of unconscious wish could such a horrific repeated dream be fulfilling? According to Freud, "It is hard to guess" (1932, *S.E.*, XXII: 28). Second, there is a relaxation of censorship in the dream work of punishment dreams. In normal dreams, underlying sexual wishes are encrypted by condensation, displacement, and other methods. Once encrypted, unconscious wishes are not expressed nakedly in consciousness. That is not the case with punishment dreams. Moreover, punishment dreams end in anxiety, not a release of pleasure (1932, *S.E.*, XXII: 28–29).

Freud acknowledged here that something has gone wrong, yet "the exception does not overturn the rule." He clarified. "We say that a dream is the fulfillment of a wish; but if you want to take these latter objections into account, you can say nevertheless that a dream is an attempt at the fulfillment of a wish." There is a failure of the dream work with "unconscious fixation to trauma." At night, relaxation of defenses allows the unconscious fixation of the trauma to surge into consciousness, but "there is failure in the functioning of his dream-work, which would like to transform the memory-traces of the traumatic event into the fulfillment of a wish." It is the same with sufficiently traumatic childhood experiences (1932, *S.E.*, XXII: 29–30). Thus Freud abandoned the second thesis of his bipartite thesis concerning dreams—not all dreams are the fulfilment of unconscious wishes—though he still clung to the notion that all dreams are generated by unconscious wishes, a claim Freud had to know was too strong, as evidenced by his hungry daughter's dream of strawberries, his dream of wanting to drink after eating anchovies, and the like, unless he was making the trivial point that one does not have conscious wishes when asleep.

Something has gone wrong with the stated etiology. Freud's explanation is problematic. Why is there need of bringing in a "punishing agency of the mind"? Might it not be that the repetition of a traumatic experience is the mind's way of coming to grips with that horrific experience? That is possible. Thus there is no need to view such dreams as a challenge to the wish-fulfillment thesis and as a problem for the economics of the pleasure principle.

Freud thought otherwise. The problem of punishment dreams arises because in *The Interpretation of Dreams*, the dream censor has a different role than has the superego in the structural model, and that role involves id, ego, and superego. Its role is to block repressed, unconscious content and to allow preconscious content. The superego, in contrast, has punitive functions. It can achieve what the dream censor cannot. It can punish bad content by punishing dreamers, for example by making the dreamer feel guilty. To the extent that Freud wished to retain the topographical theory and the structural theory, the problem becomes acute. It is telling that the structural theory's ascendance brings this puzzle into focus.[21]

That notwithstanding, the problem of traumatic neuroses would always prove pressing for him. A solution would be forthcoming not by tweaking with his model of dreams, but by a change in his metapsychology. He would propose (1920) and add (1923) a death drive to account for punishment dreams, which would become theoretically manifestations of a daemonic compulsion to repeat—the topic of chapters 4 and 5. The death drive would also, for Freud, make plausible the sadistic tendencies of the superego.

NOTES

1. That is in spite of the fact that there were no known physiological correlates. This sentiment is conveyed by Freud's metaphorical use of a crystal, thrown to the ground. When it breaks, it does not break arbitrarily, but according to lines of cleavage, predetermined by the structure of the crystal (1933, *S.E.*, XXII: 1933: 58–59).

2. For a fine account of the fin-de-siècle treatments for nervous disorders, see Sonu Shamdasani, "'Psychotherapy': The Invention of a Word," *History of the Human Sciences*, vol. 18, no. 1, 2008: 2–3.

3. See his letter to Fliess of August 29, 1888, in Sigmund Freud, *The Complete Letters of Sigmund Freud to Wilhelm Fliess: 1887–1904*, ed. Jeffrey Moussaieff Masson (Cambridge: Harvard University Press, 1985), 24, and "Preface to the Translation of Bernheim's *Suggestion*" (1888, *S.E.*, I: 97–98).

4. Sigmund Freud, *The Complete Letters of Sigmund Freud to Wilhelm Fliess*, 193.

5. Brentano writes, "Not only may physical states be aroused by physical states and mental by mental, but it is also the case that physical states have mental consequences and mental states have physical consequences." Franz Brentano, *Psychology from an Empirical Standpoint*, trans. A. C. Rancurello, D. B. Terrell, and L. L. McAllister (New York: Humanities Press, 1973), 6.

6. Anna was not cured, as Breuer wrote. Upon cessation of treatment, Breuer claimed Anna was completely cured, but he himself referred her to the famous sanitarium Bellevue in Switzerland for additional treatment years later.

7. Due it seems to his uneasiness with Anna's dependence on him, which turned sexual, during his sessions with her. For Freud's own account of his break with Breuer in his own words, see "History of the Psycho-Analytic Movement" (1914, *S.E.*, XIV: 11–12), "Autobiographical Study" (1925, *S.E.*, XX: 22–23), and "Psycho-Analysis" (1922, *S.E.*, XVIII: 237).

8. Sigmund Freud, *The Complete Letters of Sigmund Freud to Wilhelm Fliess, 1887–1904*, 61.

9. For more, see K. R. Eissler, *Freud and the Seduction Hypothesis: A Brief Love Affair* (Madison, CT: Psychosocial Press, 2001).

10. Freud wrote in a letter (1908) to disciple Karl Abraham, "The resistance to infantile sexuality strengthens me in my opinion that the three essays are an achievement of comparable value to the *Interpretation of Dreams*." Sigmund Freud, *The Letters of Sigmund Freud*, ed. Ernst Freud (London: The Hogarth Press, 1961), 145.

11. Sigmund Freud, *The Letters of Sigmund Freud*, ed. Ernst Freud (New York: Basic Books, 1961).

12. Translated consistently by Strachey as "instinct." We leave unaltered Strachey's translational preference in all quotes.

13. A term first employed by Freud in 1910. For more, see Peter Hartcollis, "Origins and Evolution of the Oedipus Complex as Conceptualized by Freud," *Psychoanalytic Review*, vol. 92, no. 3, 2005, 315–34.

14. The implausibility of putting so much weight on sexuality is not hard to spot. Consider a line of inquiry elaborated by the renegade analyst John Bowlby. Bowlby is an early culmination of a line of psychoanalytic inquiry linked to Winnicott that stressed that a failure of good enough mothering can lead to pathologies in attachment. John Bowlby, *Attachment: Attachment and Loss*, vol. 1 (New York: Basic Books, 1999). Bowlby's is a clear-cut articulation of a line of inquiry that started with the Object Relations theorists. But even Freud himself has clear deviations from this type of thinking. In particular, "Mourning and Melancholia" (1917, *S.E.*, XIV: 237–58) does not fit the sexual etiology account of neurosis. Freud felt no need to cling to bold hypotheses when it came to details. Sletvold shows how Freud Psychic trauma and defense theory to a sexual trauma seduction theory, to a sexual trauma theory to explain neurosis. Sletvold argues that it is the first theory that does the best job of explaining neurosis, and that seduction and the sexual or libido theory are unsuccessful. J. Sletvold, "Freud's Three Theories of Neurosis: Towards a Contemporary Theory of Trauma and Defense," *Psychoanalytic Dialogues*, vol. 26 (2016), 460–75.

15. The obvious comparison is foreplay in sex.

16. For a complete account of the Oedipus complex in this and other of Freud's works, see M. Andrew Holowchak, "Freud's Oedipus Complex: Shibboleth or Canard?" *Radical Claims in Freudian Psychoanalysis: Point/Counterpoint* (Lanham, MD: Jason Aronson, 2012).

17. One important note: Freud's view on the onset of neurosis changed over time, as he grappled with "the choice of neurosis." In earlier writings, he settled on the view that neurosis was determined by the period of time in which the sexual trauma occurred—"by the time of its genesis"—but later, he settled on the time of repression.

18. Gerasimos Santas, *Plato and Freud: Two Theories on Love* (New York: Basil Blackwell, 1988, 105).

19. Freud thought religious ritual was essentially obsessive. The differences are that religious ritual lacks the diversity of individual obsessional neurosis and that religious ritual is publicly practiced (1907, *S.E.*, IX: 118–19).

20. See Patrick J. Mahony, *Freud and the Rat Man* (New Haven, CT: Yale University Press, 1986), and Frank Sulloway, "Reassessing Freud's Case History: The Social Construction of Psychoanalysis," *Isis*, Vol. 82, No. 2, 1991, 245–75.

21. Further elaboration of the defense also can show similar phenomena. There are an indefinitely large number of ways to defend against emerging drive derivatives. Not all of them need prevent conscious acknowledgment of a wish or impulse. Instead, one might as it were deny it is one's own thought, one might project it, one might even scold oneself for having so nasty a wish, but assert that my hating myself for coveting my neighbor's wife is proof that it is not a real wish of mine.

Chapter Two

Repetition and Neurosis: Phylogenetic Account

The previous chapter offered a look at the role of "repetition" in psychoanalysis. In this chapter, we look at Freud's attempt to ground historically, and biologically, his ontogenetic views. This phylogenetic grounding, as it were, is itself based on repetition—the recapitulationism made prominent by Ernst Haeckel—"ontogeny recapitulates phylogeny"[1]—which Freud found tantalizing and from which, time and time again, he drew in an effort to give his psychology a biological support in human history, even though the doctrine has ceased to be part of modern biological science.[2] The biology here, as we shall see, is Lamarckian, not Darwinian.

Our focus in this chapter covers some of Freud's strangest phylogenic speculations in letters and published and unpublished materials. That said, our focus is not condemnation. Our focus is historical, not critical. We aim to show how Freud's desire for completeness of etiological explanation led him to entertain some rather unsavory and maverick views, of questionable relevance to psychoanalysis. He is, as we show in these phylogenetic musings, driven again by the notion of repetition.

"AN EXPERIENCE . . . COMMON TO ALL HUMAN BEINGS"

Having discussed three neuroses in which repetition is critical, there is an etiological problem. If (usually early sexual) experiences cause neuroses, then what is an analyst to make of generic or typical symptoms of different neuroses? Can there be such things?

Freud expressed optimism. "If the individual symptoms are so unmistakably dependent on the patient's experience, it remains possible that the typical symptoms may go back to an experience which was in itself typical—common to all human beings." Freud is referring to typical dreams—dreams of falling, flying, floating, swimming, being inhibited, and being naked—whose symbols indicate but one interpretation, though that interpretation may be trumped by appeal to the dreamer's circumstances, gleaned through associations (1917, *S.E.*, XVI: 271–72).

Freud can be read as hinting at phylogenic counterparts to ontogenetic experiences—thereby making the ontogenetic experiences repetitions of events critical in the development of the human species.

What are those phylogenic counterparts? In *Three Essays on Sexuality*, Freud wrote that there is a relationship between ontogeny and phylogeny. "Ontogenesis may be considered as a repetition of phylogenesis insofar as the latter has not been varied by a more recent experience. The phylogenetic disposition makes itself visible behind the ontogenetic process." What happens ontogenetically is just "the precipitate of a former experience of the species to which the newer experience of the individual being is added as the sum of the occasional factors" (1905, *S.E.*, VII: xii).

How does that relate to the Oedipus complex? We need to say more about the Oedipus complex before proceeding.

Freud first mentioned "Oedipus" in a letter to Wilhelm Fliess (15 Oct. 1897).

> I have found, in my own case too, being in love with my mother and jealous of my father, and I now consider it a universal event in early childhood. . . . The Greek legend seizes upon a [repetitive] compulsion which everyone recognizes because he senses its existence within himself. Everyone in the audience was once a budding Oedipus in fantasy and each recoils in horror from the dream fulfillment here transplanted into reality, with the full quantity of repression which separates his infantile state from his present one.

"It is the fate of all of us, perhaps, to direct our first sexual impulse towards our mother and our first hatred and our first murderous wish against our father" (1900, *S.E.*, IV: 297), said Freud in Chapter 5 of *Interpretation of Dreams*, where he introduced the Oedipus story as a factor in psycho sexuality. It is not the futility of trying to escape our fate that grips us, but instead Oedipus' particular fate. Being in love with one parent and hating the other is the principal part of the lives of children who become psychoneurotic. Escaping that situation in the right manner is as close to psychical normalcy as one can get. In ordinary development, a child's first passions are directed at the mother and father, or their functional equivalents.

Freud first introduced "Oedipus complex" ten years later in "Special Type of Object-Choice Made by Men." Desire for his mother and thirst for revenge against his father are the boy's two driving forces. He finds refuge in diverse masturbatory fantasies of his mother, who seems to him an unfaithful partner. "The lover with whom she commits her act of infidelity," Freud added, "almost always exhibits the features of the boy's own ego, or more accurately, of his own idealized personality, grown up and so raised to a level with his father" (1910, *S.E.*, XI: 171).

Three years later, in *Totem and Taboo* in 1913, Freud explained neurosis as infantile fixation or infantile regression that is oedipal. "We have arrived," Freud proclaimed, "at the point of regarding a child's relation to his parents, dominated as it is by incestuous longing, as the nuclear complex of neurosis." He appealed to oedipal longings in creative writing and in the taboo of incest by savages. The modern-day taboo of incest, he conjectured, has its origins in totemic law, which prohibits the killing of the totem animal and prohibits sexual intercourse with members of the opposite sex in the same totem clan (1913, *S.E.*, XIII: 32).

Freud gave a lengthy elaboration of the Oedipus complex, critical to the "psycho-analytic explanation of the neuroses," in *Introductory Lectures* (1917, *S.E.*, IX: 329–38). Observation shows that all pubescent children have intense oedipal impulses, but they remain outside of consciousness. However, as an adolescent, a child must separate himself from his parents before he can become an independent member of human society. Seldom does detachment occur along the best line. With neurotics, there is no relevant detachment. A son, all his life, bows to his father's authority; a daughter, to her mother's. "In this sense the Oedipus complex may justly be regarded as the nucleus of all the neuroses."

What puts an end to oedipal strivings? In "Dissolution of the Oedipus Complex," where he then was working with the structural model, Freud claimed that a boy's masturbating ceases due to the threat of castration, which he takes to be genuine once he observes a naked female. Such castration anxiety, the most harrowing experience of his young life, puts an abrupt end to his longing for his mother and hatred of his father. He enters a period of sexual latency, after which the Oedipus complex is "destroyed," and through desexualization and sublimation, the superego or sense of conscience forms. The boy takes up his father's sense of morality through identification with him. In less successful cases, the libido is merely repressed and the result is neurosis (1924, *S.E.*, XIX: 175–77).

There is a similar story to be told vis-à-vis girls, who long for their father. Yet, not having a penis, there can be nothing comparable to a boy's castration threat to end a girl's lust for her father. Without an end to her lusting, there can be no latency period, no desexualization, no sublimation, and no development of a strong superego. Thus, girls grow up along different lines than boys. Girls do not have to differentiate themselves from their opposite-sex parent the way that a boy does and identify with their same-sex parent.

In "Psycho-Analysis," Freud described the significance of successful oedipal sublimation for individuals as well as the human species. "The reactions against the instinctual demands of the Oedipus complex are the source of the most precious and socially important achievements of the human mind; and this holds true not only in the life of individuals but probably also in the history of the human species as a whole" (1926, *S.E.*, XX: 268).

By 1933, the Oedipus complex convinced Freud, in "Anxiety and Instinctual Life," that his view of the etiology of hysteria is mistaken. Anxiety is a signal of emerging danger from unconscious wishes and impulses. Anxiety triggers defenses that repress the emerging material, thereby reducing (temporarily) anxiety to a tolerable level. In oedipal instances, for the boy, signal anxiety is a warning of danger. The danger might be an internalized fear of castration, leading to anxiety. "We must hold fast to the view that fear of castration is one of the commonest and strongest motives of repression and thus for the formation of neuroses" (1933, *S.E.*, XXII: 85–87), though it finds no place in women, who are motivated by loss of parental affection. Further, it may be accurate to say that unconscious fear of castration, often represented as fear of any physical injury, triggers aggressive impulsive sadistic wishes or other objectionable wishes or impulses (viz., a wish the castrator was dead or a impulse to attack the father or substitute) that lead to anxiety when they begin to emerge.

Freud in his posthumously published *Outline of Psycho-Analysis* (1940) sketched how the Oedipus complex paves the way for neurosis. The ego comes to grief over handling the real oedipal danger of castration. It is too immature to handle such dangers. He writes, "We cannot escape the conclusion that neuroses could be avoided if the childish ego were spared this task—if . . . the child's sexual life were allowed free play, as happens among many primitive peoples." Instead the ego has the task of damming up the sexual drives on account of reality and the overly strict superego (1940, *S.E.*, XXIII: 200–5). So great is this contribution to science, Freud said, that "if psycho-analysis could boast no other achievement than the discovery of the repressed Oedipus complex, that alone would give it a claim to be included among the precious new acquisitions of mankind" (1940, *S.E.*, XXIII: 191–93).

Once again this passage appeals to repetition, and to recapitulationism. The Oedipus complex itself, because of its avowed universality, cannot have an explanation grounded in the early experiences of each individual, unless each individual's formative experiences are similar. There must be some explanation for the similarities. There must be a shared history behind it—a phylogenetic explanation that has become part of our biological inheritance à la Lamarck.

Freud's earlier phylogenetic explanation—driven by the research/speculations of Darwin, Atkinson, Frazer, and Robertson Smith (1913, *S.E.*, XIII: 125–26 and 131–39)—took him back to the primal horde—the ancestral horde of all humanity. In this horde, he speculated in *Totem and Taboo*, the primal father, as the leader and the strongest male, gave free rein to his sexual impulses to the dismay of the weaker men. The impeded sexual impulses of the weak eventually provoked them to form a pact to kill the primal father—the first genuine social deed, indicative of strength through numbers. After killing the primal father, they disposed of the corpse in a cannibalistic feast.[3] The magnitude of the deed was so great that it stayed with the weak, the killers, in the form of a "forgotten" memory, passed on in Lamarckian fashion to subsequent generations (1913, *S.E.*, XIII: 140–46). Thus the ontogenetic Oedipus complex, rooted in wishing, has as its origin a phylogenetic deed—a fulfilled wish, an actual patricide.[4]

Freud acknowledged "grave difficulties" with his "deduction" to the primal deed in *Totem and Taboo* (1913, *S.E.*, XIII: 158), but by the time of *Moses and Monotheism*, over twenty-five years later, the grave difficulties are gone and the deed now must have been repeated—viz., it must have been committed numerous times in numerous hordes in early human history. "Since the emergence of the idea of [Lamarckian] evolution no longer leaves room for doubt that the human race has a prehistory, and since this is unknown—that is, forgotten—a conclusion of this kind [i.e., the primal deed] almost carries the weight of a postulate" (1939, *S.E.*, XXIII: 80), a sly admission that it has not been established by the weight of evidence.

Strangely enough, in *Moses and Monotheism*, Freud found confirmation of the phylogenetic component of the Oedipus complex in two other ways. First, there are the reactions of patients to early trauma. Often such a reaction, especially in the cases of the Oedipus and castration complexes, is incompatible with what a subject has actually experienced, but "fits in much better with the model of a phylogenetic event and, in general, can only be explained by such an influence." The evidential value of such an archaic event is strong enough for Freud to posit that the archaic heritage comprises both dispositions and (fantastical) memory-traces of the killing of the primal father. Second, there is a pragmatic justification. "If we assume the survival of these memory-traces in the archaic heritage, we have bridged the gulf between individual and group psychology: we can deal with peoples as we do with an individual neurotic." In this, human beings are the same as other animals. He summed up, "I have no hesitation in declaring that men have always known (in this special way) that they once possessed a primal father and killed him" (1939, *S.E.*, XXIII: 99–101). Both "confirmations" are, of course, classroom-type examples of confirmation bias, and the argument is therefore patently fallacious. It also seems to have no obvious clinical consequences.

In *Civilization and Its Discontents*, Freud noted a role for repetition in sustaining guilt. Guilt is an ontogenetic repetition of the phylogenic past in that it goes back to the killing of the primal father. The remorse associated with historic murder was the result of a patient's own memory traces of primal ambivalence toward the primal father. Through hatred, the sons committed the deed; through love, they came to experience remorse. Remorse resulted in internalizing the father's power through establishing conscience and through restrictions against any repetition of the murder or its psychic equivalents. "And since the inclination to aggressiveness against the father was *repeated* in the following generations, the sense of guilt, too, persisted, and it was reinforced once more by every piece of aggressiveness that was suppressed and carried over to the superego" (1930, *S.E.*, XXI: 132–33). The unhappy aspect of Freud the social theorist is that when he detaches himself from clinical considerations, he has a tendency to forgo familiar constraints on theorizing like conservatism, modesty, simplicity, generality, and refutability.[5]

GROUNDING THE Ψ NEUROSES

In a strange letter, published posthumously, to Sandor Ferenczi, Freud speculated that different forms of neuroses have different phylogenic antecedents. The letter, written on July 12, 1915, begins as follows: "There is a series of chronological starting points in patients which runs thus: Anxiety hysteria—conversion hysteria—obsessional neurosis—dementia praecox—paranoia—melancholia-mania. . . . This series seems to repeat phylogenetically an historical origin. What are now neuroses were once phases in human conditions."[6]

The first triad of neuroses concerns problems with glaciation and relate to the three transference neuroses. First, privations in the pre-speech glacial period made men apprehensive and transformed libido into *anxiety*. Second, they realized that there must be certain restrictions to propagation and that led to *hysteria*. Third, with the development of speech and intelligence, primal hordes were formed and the primal father forced libidinal prohibitions. Compulsion, qua *obsessional neurosis*, marked their struggle to return to the former state, an impossible scenario, and the resulting neuroses were acquired by the sons in a Lamarckian, rather than Darwinian, manner.

The second triad of neuroses "belong to a new epoch and were acquired by the sons." These concern the sons' relationship to their primal father prior to and after his murder, and relate to the three narcissistic neuroses. We continue Freud's account. Fourth, the sons were forced to relinquish all sexual objects by threat of castration, and the result was dementia praecox (schizophrenia). Fifth, the sons, driven out by the father, organized themselves on a homosexual basis and their struggle with their homosexuality was signified by *paranoia*. Finally, they killed the father, mourned him, and effected an identification with him and the result was mania-melancholia.[7]

The letter points to an unpublished metapsychological manuscript, "Overview of the Transference Neuroses"—the twelfth of twelve Freud had intended to write in a book to be titled *Preliminaries to a Metapsychology*.

Ferenczi's reply to Freud's letter was brief—too brief for Freud, who subsequently chided his friend (18 July 1915). Ferenczi wrote back concerning Freud's "phylogenetic fantasy," and added, perhaps to placate Freud, that the notion is "extraordinarily seductive." He also articulated devastating objections, one of which is that the fixation of the castrated sons cannot have been acquired, as castrated sons cannot reproduce. After a few more letters exchanged, Freud mentioned that his last metapsychological essay is completed and that his publisher, Hugo Heller, has consented to publish the book of metapsychological essays.[8]

Freud abandoned the metapsychological book and published only five of the essays intended for it. The other seven were lost but the twelfth essay was later found in a trunk by Ilse Grubrich-Simitis in 1983.[9] And so, an exploration of a draft of that unpublished essay, sent to Ferenczi on July 28, 1915, is profitable as it sheds light on his employment of "repetition," his attachment to recapitulationism, and his enduring wish to give his psychology a metapsychological or biological grounding.

Referring to his "Two Principles of Mental Functioning" (1911), Freud said that the ego-strivings develop differently from the sex strivings, as the former, object-directed, aim at reality. Libido's path is repetitive, and archaic. "One thereby gets the impression that the developmental history of the libido recapitulates a much older piece of the development than that of the ego; the former perhaps recapitulates conditions of the phylum of vertebrates, whereas the latter is dependent on the history of the human race."[10]

Freud cited two sources of inspiration to explain the transference neuroses. First, Fritz Wittels posited a primeval paradise in which all human needs were satisfied, and Freud added there would have been no need for "periodicity of the libido." Next, he followed Ferenczi, who conjectured that the development of those primal humans was stimulated by the Ice Age to civilize, or perish. And so the dispositions to anxiety hysteria, obsessional neurosis, and conversion hysteria are part of a "regression to phases that the whole human race had to go through at some time from the beginning to the end of the Ice Age." In that regard, the transference neuroses, experienced by some people today, are manifestations of their hereditary tendency along with new acquisitions.[11]

With the privations brought about by the encroaching ice age, humans became anxious, as the hitherto friendly world turned hostile, parlous. The anxiety however was realistic, a response to actual danger, not imagined, but the privations paved the way for ontogenetic anxiety hysteria. With human existence threatened, there must have been a conflict between self-preservation and desire to procreate, with diminished probability of preservation in tough times. Lack of procreation led to perverse gratification of impulses. Such tension, Freud says, typically leads to hysteria. Last, with degradation of man's "sexual activity to an earlier phase," intelligence was needed. Man developed language in some attempt to master the hostile world. Acquisition of language made man—here he has in mind the primal father—both feel that "he was himself invulnerable and that his possession of women must not be challenged." Thus this early phase was characterized by obsessional neurosis, as there exist "the overemphasis on thinking, the enormous energy that returns in the [repetitive] compulsion, the omnipotence of thoughts, [and] the inclination to inviolable laws."[12] Of course the argument will strike contemporary readers as a tissue of speculation, to put it kindly, or a tissue of nonsense, to put it accurately.

Freud then turned to narcissistic neuroses. "The disposition to them had been acquired by a second generation, whose development introduces a new phase of human civilization."[13]

First, following the story in *Totem and Taboo* (1913), the primal father of the early horde drove out the sons when they were pubescent. Yet here Freud added that he robbed them of their manhood, so that they could "stay with the horde as harmless laborers." The effect of castration, again actual, extinguished the libido and left individual development at a standstill. That is what happens with dementia praecox, which leads to "giving up every love-object, degeneration of all sublimations, and return to auto-eroticism," as if he has been castrated.[14]

Next the threatened sons flew from the horde to avoid castration and allied among themselves to enhance survival, and thus formed the first social bands through homosexual attachments. "This phase of the condition, however, manifestly brings back paranoia; more correctly, paranoia defends itself against its return. . . . Paranoia tries to ward off homosexuality, which was the basis for the organization of brothers, and in so doing must drive the victim out of society and destroy his social sublimations."[15]

Finally, and at long last, Freud confessed that it is hard to place melancholia-mania, but it must belong to "the age of maturity." The sons banded together and killed the primal father, and then there was "triumph over his death, then mourning over the fact that they all still revered him as a model." He added, "The mourning of the primal father proceeds from identification with him, and such identification we have established as the prerequisite for the melancholic mechanism."[16]

Thus the human vulnerability to the transference neuroses was acquired "in the struggle with the exigencies of the Ice Age," while our disposition to the narcissistic neuroses was acquired from the sexual "oppression by the father." The first struggle led "to the patriarchal stage of civilization"; the last, "to the social"; but "from both came the fixations which in their return after millennia became the disposition of the two groups of neuroses." It is in this phylogenetic sense of acquisition that we can call neurosis "a cultural acquisition,"[17] and individual neuroses repetitions of that acquisition.

Here Freud reminded his readers, as if they needed reminding, that the ontogenetic/phylogenetic parallel might be no more than a "playful comparison." He said, "The extent to which it may throw light on the still unsolved riddles of the neuroses should properly be left to further investigation, and illumination through new experiences."[18] And so, these wild speculations about human history require clinical corroboration. Freud would have done well to have considered what would refute them as well.

Freud soon had doubts about the series of metapsychological essays. He published five in journals, and let the others sit. Grubrich-Simitis writes, "He no longer regarded what had been set forth in the seven unpublished papers as a successful synthesis of his theoretical conceptions."[19] He decided against publishing the book. The reason cannot be definitively known, but it is likely that the collection was too speculative—too untethered from clinical work from actual psychoanalyses of actual patients. He admitted in a subsequent letter to Ferenczi that the phylogenetic account is "a legitimate complement and necessary consequence of my views on the Ψ." Yet, to his credit, he immediately added, "One should not make theories—they must fall into one's house as uninvited guests while one is occupied with the investigation of details."[20]

And so, Freud became convinced that inference to the series of chronological starting points for the Ψ neuroses was too neat, and thus, best left to fantasy, especially in light of its remoteness from clear-cut clinical observation. Still, we ought not to be too critical of Freud. He never stated that the theory expounded in the essay was more than a "phylogenetic fantasy" that awaited future confirmation or would serve as a heuristic. Still, as we have noted earlier, the theoretical fantasy offers another illustration of the fundamental role of "repetition" in psychoanalytic theory. It also exemplifies Freud's fondness for recapitulationism and the importance of giving his psychology a metapsychological or pseudo-biological grounding in the play of human history.

Nonetheless, having faith that there were strong parallels between the development of individuals and that of the species over time, Freud would later in life apply his psychoanalytic findings vis-à-vis individual pathology to groups. That occurs prominently in works such as *Group Psychology and the Analysis of the Ego* (1921), *The Future of an Illusion* (1927), and *Civilization and Its Discontents* (1930). In that way, therapy that was directed at enabling individuals to gain a greater sense of unity through recapturing their own history, instead of reliving it through repetitive pathological symptoms. In that manner, psychoanalysis could be directed, at least prophylactically, at groups. Thus, the aim of group psychology, to be distinguished from group therapy that does focus on psychoanalytic processes, can be grasped as giving all human beings a greater awareness of their own species' history to prevent them, to paraphrase Santayana, from repeating it. Scharfenberg writes: "If Freud . . . tried to free the patient from precisely the vicious circle of the constant compulsion to repeat, then that was also true for the phenomenal forms of culture: if history exhausts itself in constant repetition, it maintains a pathological character trait. . . . The liberation of the human race from these compulsions to repeat is, therefore, the real passion of his criticism of religion."[21]

The grand metempirical speculations covered in this chapter are, of course, shamelessly unscientific, yet the Freudian trope of repetition is unmistakable in them, and so they prove to be of historical significance. Yet such historical writings on the relationship of, for example, the vulnerability of men to the Oedipus complex or the killing of the primal father are distinct from what is often counted as metapsychology for Freud: his dynamic, economic, topographic, drive, and structural theories of the psychical apparatus. As Anna Freud puts it: "Any phenomenon can and should be described from multiple points of view to understand it. . . . The human personality is so complex that no one perspective can adequately encompass it."[22] There is, thus, room for metapsychology in psychoanalysis.[23]

Freud's recapitulationist fantasies are largely ignored today by clinicians. Why? They are mostly irrelevant to clinical work. Psychoanalysts, as all clinicians, take patients as they get them. To take a suggestion of Edelson, one can treat a patient as a "Freudian system,"[24] and get certain clinical results. One can test Freudian hypotheses and make Freudian interventions. Of course if patients are not Freudian systems, things may not go so well.

Still, one must keep in mind that effective clinical work may rest on faulty theory. For example, the Minnesota Multiphasic Personality Inventory in its various incarnations is widely used and clinically supported, even though the diagnostic categories it was initially intended to spot—for example hypochondriasis, hysteria, and psychoesthesia—have long ago been placed in the psychiatric dustbin. Instead of relating MMPI scores to defunct diagnostic categories, psychologists studied and established scoring systems within the MMPI that remain of current interest, as do MMPI profiles. So, the current justified neglect of Freud's fin de siècle natural and social sciences has made little if any difference to psychoanalytic practice. The situation is far from uncommon in clinical work.

NOTES

1. That the development of an individual over time is the same as the development of the species over time.

2. As Zilboorg correctly notes: "Freud never gave up his belief . . . that the parallel he drew between Fechner's ideas in physics and his own in human psychology was not really a parallel but an actual proof that his concept of the mental apparatus and its energy in the economic

model was actually the same as Helmholtz' and Fechner's ideas about physical energy. To this faith he clung to the last, expressing the hope that some day the whole complexity of human reactions and relations could be reduced to some as yet undiscovered physico-chemical reactions. In other words, Freud remained an *organicist* throughout his scientific life." Gregory Zilboorg, "Introduction, in Sigmund Freud, *Beyond the Pleasure Principle* (New York: W.W. Norton & Company, 1961), xxviii–xxix. For the rejection of Haeckel's doctrine, see Stephen Jay Gould, *Ontogeny and Phylogeny, New Edition*, Cambridge, MA: Harvard University Press, 1990.

3. In "Psycho-Analysis," Freud says that the main taboos of totemism—not to kill the tribal ancestor and not to marry a woman from one's own clan—correspond precisely to the two oedipal wishes—to kill one's father and marry one's mother (1923,, *S.E.*, XVIII: 253). Freud overall is aiming to explain why Christ had to die on the cross—*lex talionis*, or an eye for an eye (if Christ had to die, the sin of mankind must have been a murder)—and the Christian practice of communion (compare to the cannibalistic feast of the sons).

4. In "An Infantile Neurosis," his most complete and important case study, Freud says the Oedipus complex is one of several phylogenetically inherited schemata, where the impressions of actual experience are derived (1918, *S.E.*, XVII: 119).

5. See W. V. Quine and J. S. Ullian, *The Web of Belief* (Columbus: McGraw-Hill Education, 1978).

6. Sigmund Freud and Sandor Ferenczi, *The Correspondence of Sigmund Freud and Sandor Ferenczi*, ed. Ernst Falzeder and Eva Brabant (Cambridge: The Belknap Press, 1996), 65–66. In fairness to Freud, the clinical observation led him to notice similarities between these disorders and sequences in his biological reading.

7. This last cluster of illnesses comprises psychoses. The previous cluster, personality disorders. The first cluster are typical neuroses, which do not impair reality.

8. Sigmund Freud and Sandor Ferenczi, *The Correspondence of Sigmund Freud and Sandor Ferenczi*, 67–73.

9. Axel Hoffer and Peter T. Hoffer, "Foreword," in Ilse Grubrich-Simitis, *Sigmund Freud: A Phylogenetic Fantasy: Overview of the Transference Neuroses* (Cambridge: The Belknap Press, 1987), vii.

10. Ilse Grubrich-Simitis, *Sigmund Freud: A Phylogenetic Fantasy: Overview of the Transference Neuroses* (Cambridge: The Belknap Press, 1987), 11–12.

11. Ilse Grubrich-Simitis, *Sigmund Freud*, 13.

12. Ilse Grubrich-Simitis, *Sigmund Freud*, 13–16.

13. Ilse Grubrich-Simitis, *Sigmund Freud*, 16.

14. Freud disadvises adding speech alterations and hallucinatory storms, which characterize the illness. Ilse Grubrich-Simitis, *Sigmund Freud*, 17.

15. Ilse Grubrich-Simitis, *Sigmund Freud*, 18.

16. Ilse Grubrich-Simitis, *Sigmund Freud*, 18–19.

17. Ilse Grubrich-Simitis, *Sigmund Freud*, 19.

18. Ilse Grubrich-Simitis, *Sigmund Freud*, 19. Earlier Freud writes that though "everything has been built on very careful and arduous observation," a reader must be patient and allow criticism to retreat "in the face of fancy" and unconfirmed things to be presented, merely because "they are stimulating and open up distant vistas." Ilse Grubrich-Simitis, *Sigmund Freud*, 11.

19. Ilse Grubrich-Simitis, *Sigmund Freud*, 82.

20. Sigmund Freud and Sandor Ferenczi, *The Correspondence of Sigmund Freud and Sandor Ferenczi*, 75.

21. Johann Scharfenberg, *Sigmund Freud & His Critique of Religion* (Philadelphia: Fortress Press, 1988), 121. For a deep theory of psychoanalytic group therapy, see Wilfred R Bion, *Experiences in Groups, and other Papers*, New York: Basic Books, 1961.

22. Jack Novick and Kerry Kelly Novick, "Reclaiming the Land," *Psychoanalytic Psychology*, vol. 19, no. 2, 2002, 348–77.

23. Pine is among analysts who champion the use of metapsychology in psychoanalysis. Keeping metapsychological speculation close to observation, he offers an example of how metapsychology, unlike the speculations in books like *Moses and Monotheism*, *Totem and*

Taboo, or *Civilization and Its Discontents*, can be used, and used effectively, in clinical practice. Fred Pine, *Drive, Ego, Object, and Self: A Synthesis for Clinical Work* (New York: Basic Books, 1990).

24. Marshall Edelson. *Psychoanalysis: A Theory in Crisis*. Chicago: University of Chicago Press, 1985).

II

Beyond the Pleasure Principle and Beyond

Chapter Three

The Path to *Beyond the Pleasure Principle*

Freud's *Beyond the Pleasure Principle* was a groundbreaking work, because it marked a major shift in Freud's metapsychological thinking. Here, on account of observed "compulsions to repeat" in traumatized neurotics, Freud amended, at least provisionally, his theory of drives. Ego drives and sex drives, it seems, cannot fully account for the obsessive repetitions. Traumatized neurotics exhibit behavior that is inconsistent with and goes beyond the pleasure principle.[1]

To get to *Beyond the Pleasure Principle*, we need to go some ways toward recapitulating the path Freud created to disclose the clinical problems that led to the theoretical reshaping of his metapsychology to accommodate the daemonic compulsion to repeat and the death drive. That path, we argue, demands that we begin with repetition in dreams; examine two progenitor concepts—"repetition of what is similar" and "rediscovery of what is familiar" in *On Jokes and their Relation to the Unconscious* (1905); turn to a seminal paper, "Remembering, Repeating, and Working-Through" (1914), in which Freud introduces formally "compulsion to repeat" for in-clinic cases of severe repression; examine two substratal metapsychological essays, "On Narcissism" (1914) and "Instincts and their Vicissitudes" (1915), the first introducing a problem for the ego drives and sex drives, the latter being an ambitious attempt to flesh out the precise nature of "drive" (*Trieb*)—and end with a significant, but mostly overlooked paper, "The Uncanny" (1919), which anticipated much of what Freud would say in *Beyond the Pleasure Principle* one year later.

REPETITION AND DREAMS

One of the early uses of "repetition" occurs in translating dreams. Freud held that dreams employ *numerical multiplication* of an object to symbolize *temporal repetition.*

Chapter 6 of *The Interpretation of Dreams* describes a thirty-five-year-old male patient's dream, reported as dream at the age of four. The man as a boy lost his father one year prior to the dream, which was reported thus by Freud.

> The lawyer who had charge of his father's will . . . brought two large pears. He was given one of them to eat; the other lay on the window sill in the sitting-room.

When the boy woke up, he was convinced of the reality of his dream, and so he repeatedly asked his mother for the other pear, which he insisted was on the window sill. His mother merely laughed (1900, *S.E.*, V: 372).

Freud, of course, had much to say about the dream, which he derived through the man's associations. The boy recalled that the lawyer was a "jolly old gentleman who . . . had really once brought some pears along." The window sill of the dream was much the same as the window sill of the home. Yet the boy's mother related a dream to him. "She had had two birds sitting on her head and had asked herself when they would fly away; they did not fly away, but one of them flew to her mouth and sucked at it" (1900, *S.E.*, V: 372).

After failing to find a plausible interpretation through the method of free association, Freud turned to an "interpretation through symbolic substitution." Dream symbolism yielded the following:

> The two pears—'*pommes ou poires*'—were his mother's breasts which had given him nourishment; the window sill was the projection formed by her bosom—like balconies in dreams of houses. His feeling of reality after waking was justified, for his mother had really suckled him, and had done so, in fact, for far longer than the usual time and his mother's breast was still available to him. (1900, *S.E.*, V: 372)

How do the symbols of the dream suggest an interpretation? Freud is emphatic that this "must" be the interpretation:[2] "Give (or show) me your breast again, Mother, that I used to drink from in the past." *In the past* is symbolized by him, eating one of the pears. *Again* is symbolized by the boy's longing for the other pear. Freud asserted, "The *temporal repetition* of an act is regularly shown in dreams by the *numerical multiplication* of an object" (1900, *S.E.*, V: 373).

Yet the general rule of temporal repetition being symbolized by numerical multiplication is often ignored because of the mechanisms of the formation of dreams (and dream distortion). The mechanisms include condensation, displacement, means of representation, and secondary revision. Mechanisms of dream formation also require repetition.

Condensation refers to an economical factor in dreaming—the representation of many unconscious dream thoughts in one manifest symbol. Repetition here is involved on account of symbols being "overdetermined." Overdetermination means that a symbol in a dream tends to be ambiguous. It is a concretization of many dream thoughts, which go into the fashioning of the dream, and each symbol is determined by numerous dream thoughts. Freud wrote (1900, *S.E.*, IV: 284), "Not only are the elements of a dream determined by the dream thoughts many times over, but the individual dream thoughts are represented in the dream by several elements." Again (1901, *S.E.*, V: 652), he gave a "formula" for condensation, "Each element in the content of a dream is 'overdetermined' by material in the dream thoughts, but may be traced back to a whole number." The elements in a dream, then, are nodal points among the dream thoughts—that is, they are dream thoughts that have made their way into a dream because of their associative link with so many of the other dream thoughts. And so overdetermination is a sort of repetition. So great is the amount of condensation of almost every dream that any dream, written down, might occupy one-half sheet of paper, while the dream thoughts underlying it may occupy a "dozen times as much space." Further analysis might reveal still more meanings. So, "it is impossible to determine the amount of condensation" (1900, *S.E.*, IV: 279).

Repetition occurs often in analysis of a dream. Analysis reveals the dream thoughts giving rise to the dream. Few of those thoughts find direct expression in a dream, hence condensation. For instance, Freud's analysis of his "Botanical Monograph" dream reveals dream thoughts that lead to other thoughts, and so on, which then point back to key elements, or "nodal points," of the dream—such as "botanical" and "monograph"—which find their way into the dream. And so, the elements that have "the most numerous and strongest supports acquire the right of entry into the dream-content" (1900, *S.E.*, IV: 283–84).

Displacement is the tendency for a latent dream thought to be displaced by another thought. "The dream is, as it were, differently centred from the dream thoughts—its content has different elements as its central point" (1900, *S.E.*, IV: 305). Elsewhere, Freud added: "In the course of the dream-work the psychical intensity passes over from the thoughts and ideas to which it properly belongs on to others which in our judgement have no claim to any such emphasis. . . . In the course of this process, which I shall describe as 'dream-displacement,' the psychical intensity, significance or affective potentiality of the thought is . . . transformed into sensory vividness" (1901, *S.E.*, V: 654). Displacement is largely responsible for distortion in dreams. It softens unconscious material.

Means or considerations of representation refer to the process by which the dream work renders unconscious thoughts into conscious images. These renderings, as a "pouring of the content of a thought [unconscious] into another [visual] mold," can alter the dream even more by creating connections with other thoughts. In such manner, unrelated thoughts can merge through condensation and create the illusion of conjunction (1900, *S.E.*, V: 344). The unconscious thoughts are trains that often begin from more than one station in a network and have many points of contact. Each train is linked with a contradictory train, allowing for antinomy in interpretation. Thus the logical operators in sentences—such as *if, and, or, because*, and *just as*—cannot easily find expression in a dream. Causation can only be shown by temporal sequence. Disjunction, contrary, denial, and contradiction cannot be shown (1900, *S.E.,* IV: 315–26). Elsewhere, Freud claimed, "The manifest content of dreams consists for the most part in pictorial situations; and the dream thoughts must accordingly be submitted in the first place to a treatment which will make them suitable for a representation of this kind" (1901, *S.E.*, V: 659). The aim of means of representation is the creation of coherent wholes.

Last, there is secondary revision, which concerns material of a dream that has no correlate to the thoughts generating the dream, and is another form of repetition. Freud has us consider the dreamed critical remark, "This is only a dream." Here the censoring agency, having been "taken unawares by a dream which has already been allowed through," mobilizes against the anxiety its laxity has caused. The retort, late, is an *esprit d'escalier.* It functionally "fills up the gaps in the dream-structure with shreds and patches," is an effort to rid the dream of "absurdity and disconnectedness," and harmonizes it with "intelligible experience." This works with full, partial, or no success (1900, *S.E.,* V: 489–90).

Freud believed and was always clear that in interpreting dreams, an analyst was guided by two methods: free association and use of symbols in dreams. "The first of these procedures considers the content of the dream as a whole and seeks to replace it by another content which is intelligible and in certain respects analogous to the original one." He gave as an example Joseph's dream in the Bible of seven fat cows, and subsequently, seven lean cows that ate the fat ones—a symbol of seven years of famine in Egypt. "The second . . . might be described as the *'decoding'* method, since it treats dreams as a kind of cryptography in which each sign can be translated into another sign having a known meaning, in accordance with a fixed key." Translation occurs by reference to a dream book, in which the various elements of a dream are translated according to their assigned significance, foreboding an upcoming event, in the book (1900, *S.E.,* IV: 97–98). Freud admitted, "Serious-minded people smile at these efforts: '*Träume sind Schäume.*'"[3]

Interpretation by association, Freud asserted, is always the preferred method, for symbols need to be understood in light of a dreamer's personal experiences. Yet interpretation through symbols is useful as a means of confirming interpretation though association, filling in gaps left by association, or when associations lead nowhere (1900, *S.E.*, V: 353). Yet interpretation through symbolization is possible due to Freud's belief in recapitulationism: Ontogeny recapitulates phylogeny, or the development of an individual, from birth to death, retraces the development of the species over time—another axial use of repetition. "Things that are symbolically connected to-day were probably united in prehistoric times by conceptual and linguistic identity. The symbolic relation seems to be a relic and a mark of former identity" (1900, *S.E.*, V: 352). In short, the fixed meaning of certain symbols exists because such symbols have been passed on psycho biologically, in Lamarckian fashion, in the unconscious. That process is repeated ontogenically—hence, the possibility of interpreting symbols in dreams.

Finally, there are recurrent dreams, an obvious form of repetition. They are strangely given short shrift in a work of such magnitude. Freud referred to them on only six occasions in his magnum opus, and once in his booklet *On Dreams*, where he wrote (31), "A repetition of similar experiences [in dreams] may lead us to suspect that there is an intimate and regular relation between the unintelligible and confused nature of dreams and the difficulty of reporting the thoughts behind them." The sentiment is that recurrent dreams are evidence of their meaningfulness.

In *The Interpretation of Dreams*, he described a recurrent dream—and Freud denied having had one—as a dream that first finds expression in childhood and then "constantly reappears from time to time during adult sleep" (1900, *S.E.*, IV: 190). In chapter 6, Freud provided the example of an unpleasant recurrent dream of a certain Peter Rosegger.

> I was always a journeyman tailor and that I spent so long a time as such with my master and worked without pay in his workshop. I knew well enough, as I sat like that beside him, sewing and ironing, that my right place was no longer there and that as a townsman I had other things to occupy me. But I was always on vacation, I was always having summer holidays, and so it was that I sat beside my master as his assistant. It often irked me and I felt sad at the loss of time in which I might well have found better and more useful things to do. Now and then, when something went awry, I had to put up with a scolding from my master, though there was never any talk of wages. Often, as I sat there with bent back in the dark workshop, I thought of giving notice and taking my leave. Once I even did so; but my master paid no heed and I was soon sitting beside him again and sewing. (1900, *S.E.*, IV: 473–74)

Rosseger noted that in a subsequent variation of the dream, his master voices displeasure at his work, takes on another apprentice, which pushes him down the bench, and still another, for whom there is no room on the bench. The master dismisses him. "You've no gift for tailoring, you can go! You're dismissed!" Upon being dismissed by his master in the dream, the dream never again occurred (1900, *S.E.*, IV: 473–75).

Freud was brief about the dream. That is unexpected, given that it is quite an extraordinary recurrent dream and given that Rosseger ceases to have it after having been dismissed by his master. There is much that one can say about the elements of the dream, including the dreamer's ardent desire to quit his apprenticeship and move on to more significant, fruitful tasks. Something keeps pulling him back to the dreary backwater of a workshop, and Freud is likely right to assert that the dream is essentially masochistic. It is also noteworthy that the recurrent dream ceases only after the master dismisses his apprentice in the last dream. In Freud's report of the dream, it seems impossible for the dreamer to quit of his own choosing. Guilt at some level may be at play. The apprentice can be guilt-free, and free, only when he is dismissed by his master.

Freud did say that it is difficult to see the dream as an instance of his wish-fulfillment hypothesis: Every dream is generated by and is the fulfillment of an early childhood (usually sexual) wish (1900, *S.E.*, IV: 121–22). Freud called such dreams, distinct from wish-fulfilment dreams, "punishment dreams"—though he does not believe they pose a problem for his wish-fulfillment thesis[4] (1900, *S.E.*, V: 476). As we shall see, he later changed his mind.

Repetition of What Is Similar

Five years later, Freud appealed to "repetition" in *Jokes and their Relation to the Unconscious*. Jokes make their point through repetition. "Where the comic of situation operates by means of repetitions, it is based on the child's peculiar pleasure in constant repetition (of questions or of being told stories) which make him a nuisance to the adult" (1905, *S.E.,* V: 226). A joke is a regression, and repetition is key to what we find comical.

Freud illustrated the idea of a joke as a regression with as a key to the comical through a story of Mark Twain. Twain's brother, so goes the story, bought a bed, table, and lamp and a large sailcloth, with a hole in its middle, to act as a roof. When the hut was completed, a cow being driven fell through the hole and on the table, and thereby put out the lamp. The same thing happened the next night, the following night, and so on. After the forty-sixth night, his brother remarked, "The thing's beginning to get monotonous" (1905, *S.E.,* V: 231).

Repetition also plays a role in telling a joke. In doing so, the joker becomes convinced of the success of the joke, he derives pleasure from the laughter of the other person, and telling the joke—"where it is a question of repeating a joke that one has not produced oneself"—provides a sort of substitutive pleasure for the teller not having fashioned the joke (1905, *S.E.,* V: 156). Even if the joker authored the joke, he could derive no pleasure in it by himself. "A joke . . . *must* be told to someone else. The psychical process of constructing a joke seems not to be completed when the joke occurs to one: something remains over which seeks, by communicating the idea, to bring the unknown process of constructing the joke to a conclusion" (1905, *S.E.,* V: 143). A joke thus is something that is born only when repeated.

Thus jokes appear to be similar to dreams. Both employ condensation, displacement, and indirect representation. In a joke, as in a dream, "a sum of psychical energy which has hitherto been used for cathexis is allowed free discharge." Somebody hearing a joke "laughs with the quota of psychical energy which has become free through the lifting of the inhibitory cathexis" (1905, *S.E.,* V: 147–48). "Does not this agreement suggest the conclusion that joke-work and dream-work must, at least in some essential respect, be identical?" (1905, *S.E.,* V: 165).

Freud also in this book introduced "rediscovery of what is familiar" (*Wiederfinden des Bekannten*) or "repetition of what is similar" (*Wiederholung des Uhulichseit*)—a precursor to "compulsion to repeat," though one working with the pleasure principle—in his book on jokes, when he turns to an analysis of play as a first step in getting at the meaning of jokes.

Play appears early in childhood, with the acquisition of language, and serves the pleasure principle.

> Play—let us keep to that name [instead of "games"]—appears in children while they are learning to make use of words and to put thoughts together. This play probably obeys one of the drives which compel children to practice their capacities. In doing so, they come across pleasurable effects, which arise from a repetition of what is similar, a rediscovery of what is familiar, similarity of sound, etc.,[5] and which are to be explained as unsuspected economies in psychical expenditure. It is not to be wondered at that these pleasurable effects encourage children in the pursuit of play and cause them to continue it without regard for the meaning of words or the coherence of sentences. *Play* with words and thoughts, motivated by certain pleasurable effects of economy, would thus be the first stage of jokes (1905, *S.E.,* VIII: 128).

Games, as a regulated form of play, intensify the joy of recognition, a form of repetition, by "putting obstacles in its way"—thereby creating a damming-up that is released through that act of recognition. Thus Freud rejects the view, put forth by Karl Groos in *Die Spiele der Menschen* (*The Games of Men*) that the lure of games is in overcoming a difficulty.[6] The act of recognition is "pleasurable in itself—i.e., through relieving psychical expenditure." That is the same with "rhymes, alliterations, refrains, and other forms of repeating similar verbal sounds which occur in verse." It is also probably the same with remembering, which is similar to recognition, as both are forms of repeating (1905, *S.E.*, VIII: 121–22).

In that manner, games "make use of the mechanism of damming up only in order to increase the amount of pleasure" (1905, *S.E.*, VIII: 122). The yield of pleasure on playing games, then, is proportional to the amount of psychical release, and obstacles make sense only insofar as they increase the psychical tension and potential for its release. The analogue of games Freud has in mind is that of foreplay prior to sexual intercourse.

For adults, with maturation and strengthening of the critical faculty, reality takes center stage, and play, the emissary of the inner world, has a diminished role in adult life. Thus the rediscovery or repetition of what is familiar ceases to have the bang for adults that it has for children. Reasonableness takes its place, and the heaviness of reality sharpens the critical faculty and relegates play to meaningless or absurd activity (1905, *S.E.*, VIII: 128).

Yet despite appearances, adults cannot give up play, for no source of pleasure is ever renounced. Adult play is, then, an effort to repeat the pleasure of childhood by finding a suitable substitute that does not elicit the censures of fellow adults. Thus, adults' play is a substitutive form of repetition. One has only to reflect on the role of playful sexuality in adults to multiply examples. With the play of children being unavailable, adults find release and pleasure through jokes and jests, "the meaningless combination of words or the absurd putting together of thoughts." The pleasure is heightened by having escaped the censure of the critical faculty (1905, *S.E.,* VIII: 129). And so, the meaninglessness or absurdity is a needed guise for escape of censure. The critical faculty cannot censure what it cannot detect.

Later in the same work, Freud expanded his analysis of children's games. Their games typically involve another form of repetition—mimicry—i.e., observation and replication of adult's behavior. "A child's ambition aims far less at excelling among his equals than at mimicking the grown-ups." Mimicry of adults' situations, according to Freud, is a child's "best art" and what motivates most of his games (1905, *S.E.,* VIII: 227).

Adults too find a yield of pleasure through mimicry of children. Yet because adults' reasonableness disallows play in the manner of children, mimicry of children's situations is essentially a form of comic "degradation" for adults, but an unequivocal source of pleasure for children. "This relief, which gives the child pure pleasure, becomes in adults, in the form of degradation, a means of making things comic and a source of comic pleasure. As regards unmasking, we know that it goes back to degradation" (1905, *S.E.,* VIII: 227).

"Creative Writers and Daydreaming," three years later, shows that fantasying, which is most frequently sexual, is another sort of repetition for Freud. The seriousness of adulthood is explicable through recognition that no one succeeds in ever giving up anything that he has come to experience as pleasurable. Apparent renunciations of a childhood pleasures are in fact substitutions and, thus, covert repetition. Though one can no longer play as a child, one can fantasize on archaic preoccupations. The seriousness of adulthood is ameliorated by indulgence in repetitive daydreaming concerning fantasies, rooted in childhood (1908, *S.E.*, IX: 144).

The fantasies of adulthood, as repetitive substitutes for the play of children, are not directly recognizable to other adults. A child may play a game, whose "rules" are known only to himself—or to himself and other children—but the game he plays is not played with the intention of concealment from others. However, concealment is an indispensable part of the fantasies of an adult, who, because of shame, would rather admit his foulest misdeeds than his fantasies to another adult (1908, *S.E.*, IX: 144–45). The suggestion here is that the games that adults do play—or those aspects of them they find most pleasurable—offer clues, through substitutive repetitions, to their fantasies, rooted in childhood wishes and impulses.

The key difference between children's play and adults' daydreams lies in the motives of each. Children's play, like their dreams, is naked. It is determined by a single, unconcealed wish—to be and act like an adult—which allows for pleasure through libidinal release. Adults' daydreams, revealed to Freud in psychoanalyses, are otherwise. Constrained to act with due consideration for the real world, adults are prohibited from playing in the manner of children. Instead they resort to fantasy (1908, *S.E.*, IX: 146). A paradox is manifest. Children's play, through repeating the behaviors of adults, directly reveals their wishes to be adults. Adults' hidden fantasies, through repeating things found pleasurable as children, conceal their wishes to be, once again, children.

"REMEMBERING, REPEATING, AND WORKING THROUGH"

Freud's first use of "compulsion to repeat" (*Wiederholungszwang*) occurs in 1914 in his paper "Remembering, Repeating, and Working-Through," where he pointed out a clinical, compulsive use of *Wiederholung*—a non-daemonic signal of heightened repression. This is a watershed paper for Freud, because psychoanalytic technique prior to 1914 relied so much on remembering. Here Freud recommends a technique for working through instances of massive repression where memories through free association are not readily available. Yet clues to the repressed unconscious content in such instances are readily available through repeated behaviors in the clinical setting. What patients cannot "remember," it seems, they repeatedly act out. So to an "impulsion to remember," Freud contrasted a "compulsion to repeat."[7]

Freud began with a discussion of "forgetting." The techniques of psychoanalysis have been designed precisely with the aim of disclosing forgotten affect-saturated thoughts. Yet such forgotten thoughts are not forgotten in the ordinary manner. They are forgotten because they are inaccessible to conscious thought and need to be made available to consciousness (1914, *S.E.*, XII: 148).

Childhood amnesia—"which is theoretically so important to us"—is of particular significance. That amnesia is counterbalanced by screen memories, vivid but innocuous recollections from childhood that seem real to a person and, innocuous, often protect the person from a forgotten traumatic event. "Not only *some* but *all* of what is essential from childhood has been retained in these memories. . . . They represent the forgotten years of childhood as adequately as the manifest content of a dream represents the dream thoughts" (1914, *S.E.*, XII: 148).

Yet there are other psychical phenomena—Freud listed fantasies, processes of reference, emotional impulses, and thought connections—which must be dealt with separately from impressions and experiences. Here "forgetting" is senseless, as those phenomena were never conscious. Yet that matters little in the course of analysis, for a patient behaves much the same whether something has once been conscious and relegated to unconsciousness or something has never been conscious (1914, *S.E.*, XII: 149).

Such things noted, there are instances when, through therapy, a patient remembers nothing of what was forgotten and repressed. He merely acts it out. "He reproduces it not as a memory but as an action; he *repeats* it, without, of course, knowing that he is repeating it" (1914, *S.E.*, XII: 150). In sum, the patient is not giving his analyst a verbal repetition, but a physical one.

Freud provided an example of acting out, and nowadays, reenactment. A patient behaves defiantly and critically toward his analyst, but fails to remember that that is how he used to behave toward his parents. He produces a mass of confused dreams and associations and complains of constant failure, but does not remember that his infantile sexual life was helpless and hopeless. Rather he states that he is ashamed of his need for analytic treatment and of being now found out, and is oblivious to his terror of having his early sexual experiences and shame over them disclosed.

When his analyst informs or reminds him of the first rule of psychoanalysis—free association—the patient's associations evaporate and he is silent. His silence however is a repetition—a symptom of infantile silence and shame. "This [silence] is merely a repetition of a homosexual attitude which comes to the fore as a resistance against remembering anything." Yet his silence is a defensive resistance to the repressed material and a sign of negative transference. Freud drew the lesson, "As long as the patient is in the treatment he cannot escape from this compulsion to repeat; and in the end we understand that this is his way of remembering" (1914, *S.E.*, XII: 150).

What is the relationship between the compulsion to repeat and transference and resistance? First, transference (*Uebertragung*) itself, Freud noted, is a "piece of repetition," as the repetition is not only a transference of the forgotten past on to the analyst, but also on to other aspects of the analytic situation. "The patient yields to the compulsion to repeat, which now replaces the impulsion to remember, not only in his personal attitude to his doctor but also in every other activity and relationship which may occupy his life at the time." Second, resistance is straightforwardly related to the compulsion to repeat. He claimed, "The greater the resistance, the more extensively will acting out (repetition) replace remembering." For instance, a patient might begin therapy with "mild and unpronounced positive transference," but that scenario often changes. "The transference becomes hostile or unduly intense and therefore in need of repression," and then "remembering at once gives way to acting out." Thereafter, "the resistances determine the sequence of the material which is to be repeated," as the patient brings out weapons "of the armory of the past" to resist and combat the forward movement of treatment. Freud summed, "We have learnt that the patient repeats instead of remembering, and repeats under the conditions of resistance" (1914, *S.E.*, XII, 150–1).

Just what does a patient repeat through acting out? "He repeats everything that has already made its way from the sources of the repressed into his manifest personality—his inhibitions and unserviceable attitudes and his pathological character-traits. He also repeats all his symptoms in the course of the treatment" (1914, *S.E.*, XII: 151).

What have we learned through acting out as a repetition—as a "compulsion to repeat"? A therapist must treat a patient's illness not as a past, but as a present event (1914, *S.E.*, XII: 151–52). The scenario suggests straightforwardly the temporal direction for therapy: An analyst must work from present symptoms to their secret archaic representations in the patient. It also shows the defects of the earlier cathartic treatment, which did not focus on childhood. In cases of neurosis—going back to repressed, early childhood experiences—an analyst is guided more by repeating than remembering. Freud mentioned as an extreme case an elderly woman in the habit of fleeing her husband and house at twilight to go nowhere in particular. The woman fled from therapy after only a week. The first step of an analyst, then, is to interpret and to mobilize the patient's will and to begin the lengthy process of working through repetitions toward remembering (1914, *S.E.*, XII, 154).

Given that repeating through acting out occurs in the most severe cases of repression, repeating through acting out points to the great possibility of "deterioration during treatment."

The first stages of therapy mark a change in the conscious attitude of every patient. He accepts to some degree that he is ill, whereas before, he would in the main underestimate his illness. Still he is much unaware of his neurosis—its kind and degree. Treatment is in part aimed at helping a patient find the courage to do battle with his illness. His illness must become "an enemy worthy of his mettle."

Yet acceptance often redoubles the conflicts and triggers new symptoms, previously indistinct and often seemingly intolerable. The new symptoms, caused by "deeper-lying instinctual impulses, which had not hitherto made themselves felt, may come to be 'repeated.'" Those new symptoms might also cause harm in the patient's ordinary living, which was shielded by repression. Thus, "it [resistance] seems to say: 'See what happens if I really give way to such things. Was I not right to consign them to repression?'" The young and childish especially seem to prefer any "excuse for luxuriating in their symptoms" (1914, *S.E.,* XII: 152–53).

Here transference comes much into play. "If the attachment through transference has grown into something at all serviceable, the treatment is able to prevent the patient from executing any of the more important repetitive actions and to utilize his intention to do so *in statu nascendi* as material for therapeutic work." At such a time, an analyst protects his patient by enjoining him not to make and act on any important decisions in his life, but to postpone all decisions until recovery. Other than that, he leaves to his patient "as much personal freedom as is compatible with these restrictions" (1914, *S.E.,* XII: 153).

Overall, treating cases of repetition, through transference, is a matter of "curbing the patient's compulsion to repeat and [of] turning it into a motive for remembering." He adds: "We render the compulsion harmless, and indeed useful, by giving it the right to assert itself in a definite field. We admit it into the transference as a playground in which it is allowed to expand in almost complete freedom and in which it is expected to display to us everything in the way of pathogenic instances that is hidden in the patient's mind." By giving symptoms a "transference meaning," ordinary neurosis becomes a transference neurosis, and this new condition is now accessible to psychoanalytic intervention and allows for a transition from illness to real-world functioning. "From the repetitive reactions which are exhibited in the transference we are led along the familiar paths to the awakening of the memories, which appear without difficulty, as it were, after the resistance has been overcome" (1914, *S.E.,* XII: 154–55).

TWO CRUCIAL METAPSYCHOLOGICAL PAPERS

In a significant contribution to the literature on Freud's drive theory, Edward Bibring wrote of the four steps taken by Freud to arrive at the death drive. The first step concerned positing the first drive theory—with sex drives and ego drives and with much said about the former and little said about the latter. The second step was determined by the problem of narcissism, which showed that the ego too had its share of libido and that there was a sort of neutral energy that could be directed toward objects or the ego. The third step—"hate was to be regarded as a non-libidinal reaction of the ego"—made the ego responsible for aggression. The last step involved rethinking the human mental apparatus. With addition of a structural model in conjunction with his topographical model, Freud postulated that the ego drives and sex drives were not independent, but part of a binding drive, Eros, while in opposition to Eros, there were destructive drives, aiming to destroy living things.[8]

Bibring's sketch is spot on, and in this section, we trace out steps 2 and 3 by elaboration of two key Freudian papers—"On Narcissism" (1914) and "Instincts and their Vicissitudes" (1915).

"On Narcissism" was the first step toward revision of Freud's theory of drives. He had developed the view of an ego-drive and a sex-drive, each independent of the other and each with its own impulsive energy. Yet narcissism, excessive self-loving, showed Freud that the ego had its own reservoir of libido. That made the sharp distinction between the two drives untenable. Thus, were all drives libidinal in some refined sense of "libido"?

What then happens in instances of narcissism when sex impulses do not find real-world objects?

"The libido that has been withdrawn from the external world has been directed to the ego and thus gives rise to an attitude which may be called narcissism." It is the same in illness, when a person withdraws interest from love-objects, and in sleep. "The sick man withdraws his libidinal cathexes back upon his own ego, and sends them out again when he recovers." "Sleep, too, resembles illness in implying a narcissistic withdrawal of the positions of the libido on to the subject's own self." We are forced to conclude that there is "an original libidinal cathexis of the ego," which upon maturation gives off libido to objects, but retains some libido for itself. "We see also . . . an antithesis between ego-libido and object-libido. The more of the one is employed, the more the other becomes depleted" (1914, *S.E.*, XIV: 75–76 and 82–83).

And so, "if we grant the ego a primary cathexis of libido, why is there any necessity for further distinguishing a sexual libido from a non-sexual energy of the ego-instincts? Would not the postulation of a single kind of psychical energy save us all the difficulties of differentiating an energy of the ego-instincts from ego-libido, and ego-libido from object-libido?" (1914, *S.E.*, XIV: 76)

Freud then argued that the original use of ego drives and sex drives had arisen from biology. He has merely appropriated them for psychoanalytic purposes. "I shall be consistent enough to drop this hypothesis if psychoanalytic work should itself produce some other, more serviceable hypothesis about the instincts." That as yet has not occurred. Freud also reminded us, as he occasionally does, of the provisional nature of the psychoanalytic edifice. "All our provisional ideas in psychology will presumably some day be based on an organic substructure." Thus when chemical substances are given psychological life, the analogical leap is a matter of probability. Still, "it may turn out that . . . sexual energy—libido—is only the product of a differentiation in the energy at work generally in the mind" (1914, *S.E.*, XIV: 78–79).

Freud said in "On Narcissism," based on observations that were troublesome for his theory of ego drives and sex drives, that his posits were provisional. One year later, he published "Instincts and their Vicissitudes," where he reasserted some of the claims made in "On Narcissism."

A drive is not an external stimulus, as a drive arises within an organism, not without. An external stimulus is a "single impact," which can often be disposed by a single action, such as flight. "An instinct, on the other hand, never operates as a force giving a *momentary* impact but always as a *constant* one." Thus flight is unavailing (1915, *S.E.*, XIV: 118–19).

Freud then attempted a definition of drive (*Trieb*). "Considering mental life from a *biological* point of view, an 'instinct' [*Trieb*] appears to us as a concept on the frontier between the mental and the somatic, as the psychical representative of the stimuli originating from within the organism and reaching the mind, as a measure of the demand made upon the mind for work in consequence of its connection with the body" (1915, *S.E.*, XIV: 121–22).

He considered four characteristics of drives: pressure, aim, object, and source. "By the pressure [*Drang*] of an instinct we understand its motor factor, the amount of force or the measure of the demand for work which it represents." "The aim [*Ziel*] of an instinct is in every instance satisfaction, which can only be obtained by removing the state of stimulation at the source of the instinct." "The object [*Objekt*] of an instinct is the thing in regard to which or through which the instinct is able to achieve its aim." Finally, "by the source [*Quelle*] of an instinct is meant the somatic process which occurs in an organ or part of the body and whose stimulus is represented in mental life by an instinct" (1915, *S.E.*, XIV: 122–23). That characterization is restated by Edward Bibring. "Instinct . . . is an energy which arises from the vital stratum of the mind, which has a direction that is determined inherently, which presses forward towards a particular aim and is directed somewhat loosely towards things and persons as its object. It is linked to an organ of origin as its source and to a terminal organ as the site of its satisfaction. Its satisfaction consists in the removal of those changes in the zones of excitation which accompany the instinctual tension."[9]

Later in the essay, Freud turned to the polarity of love and hate, which he tried to accommodate with the ego drives and the sex drives. "Love is derived from the capacity of the ego to satisfy some of its instinctual impulses auto-erotically by obtaining organ-pleasure." It begins narcissistically, but then "passes over on to objects." He adds, "At the first of these aims we recognize the phase of incorporating and devouring—a type of love which is consistent with abolishing the object's separate existence and which may therefore be describes as ambivalent." Object-striving then turns, at the higher stage of sadistic-analytic, to "an urge for mastery," where "injury or annihilation of the object is a matter of indifference." Only in the genital stage is there love and hate as polarities (1915, *S.E.*, XIV: 138–39).

Hate, Freud thought, is older than love—a sentiment that is consistent with his later theory of drives—as the early narcissistic ego at first repudiates the "outpouring of stimuli" of the external world. "As an expression of the reaction of unpleasure evoked by objects, it always remains in an intimate relation with the self-preservative instincts; so that sexual and ego-instincts can readily develop an antithesis which repeats that of love and hate." Yet with the domination of the ego drives early in life, "they impart the qualities of hate to the instinctual aim" (1915, *S.E.*, XIV: 139).

Here as Bibring noted, we have the third step toward the transition to the death drive.

"THE UNCANNY"

Much of what Freud has to say in *Beyond the Pleasure Principle* is anticipated in a short essay titled "The Uncanny" (*das Unheimliche*), published one year earlier. What is significant in "The Uncanny" is that the link between repetition and libido, seemngly unbreakable in earlier works, is broken.

"Uncanny" is a special sort of word in that it is both unusual and has been neglected in the aesthetical literature, which, said Freud, has focused on "feelings of a positive nature"—that is, "beauty," "attractiveness," and "sublimity."[10] It is often used to "coincide with what excites fear in general," though it is best more narrowly linked with dread and horror. Thus the "uncanny is that class of the frightening," and "which leads back to what is known of old and long familiar" (1919, *S.E.*, XVII: 219–20). As in the case of his book on jokes, this "leading back" to something old and long familiar is certainly a "rediscovery of what is familiar," and thus, a "repetition of something similar."

Yet how can it be that something old and long familiar can be uncanny, frightening?

Appealing to lexical accounts of the German adjective *heimlich*, the word usually means "belonging to the house or family," "companionable to man" (regarding animals), and "intimate, friendlily comfortable," but it can be used to have a sense identical to *unheimlich*, to mean "concealed" or "kept from sight." Grimm's dictionary says, "*From the idea of 'homelike', 'belonging to the house', the further idea is developed of something withdrawn from the eyes of strangers, something concealed, secret.*" Thus, *Heimlich* can mean mystical or allegorical knowledge, and also "withdrawn from knowledge, unconscious," or "*something hidden and dangerous*" (1919, *S.E.*, XVII: 2122–26).

After that etymological excursion, Freud turned to the story, "The Sand Man," by E. T. A. Hoffman, who has "repeatedly employed this psychological artifice with success in his fantastic narratives." The tale, which we give in gist while Freud devotes nearly four pages to its telling, begins with Nathaniel, thinking back to his youth, when he would hear a story at night about the coming of the Sand Man, a dreadful person who would throw sand into the eyes of boys and girls, who were unwilling to go to bed. Heads bleeding from the sand, the children would then be thrown into sacks and carried to the Half-Moon as food for his children. The children of the Half-Moon, with hooked beaks, would then sit in their nest and peck at the eyes of the naughty children (1919, *S.E.*, XVII: 227–30).

Psychoanalytic experience of patients, Freud reported, shows that the fear of losing one's eyes or of damage to them is for children horrific. Analysis of dreams, myths, and fantasies demonstrates a link between that fear and the fear of castration. Oedipus' self-blinding, for illustration, was merely "a mitigated form of the punishment of castration"—the only apposite punishment by *lex talionis.*, Only the dread of castration can give the dread of losing other organs "its intense colouring." Such a connection is needed to tie together elements of the story that otherwise would appear meaningless. Thus the uncanny in Hoffman's story gets its dread from the "castration complex of childhood" (1919, *S.E.*, XVII: 231–33).

Freud continued by mining Hoffman's *The Devil's Elixir*, a work fraught with elements of the uncanny. A peculiarity of the story is the repetition of personages, features, character traits, crimes, and names over generations. That doubling, argued by Rank to be an insurance against death—e.g., the notion of a soul as a doubling of the body was an insurance against death—takes on new meaning for Freud. The doubling, as a repetition, is merely the expression of our primary narcissism, which gets surmounted when the uncanny becomes a "harbinger of death" (1919, *S.E.*, XVII: 234–36).

Yet when primary narcissism has been surmounted, the doubling does not wholly disappear. There is a doubling of the ego—the development of a critical agency that sets itself apart from and presides over the ego (i.e., the ego-ideal, or superego later) and is at least partly responsible for the factor of repetition. There is an "urge toward defence which has caused the ego to project that material outward as something foreign to itself" (1919, *S.E.*, XVII: 235–36).

In all cases of doubling, there is something uncanny. "They are a harking-back to particular phases in the evolution of the self-regarding feeling, a regression to a time when the ego had not yet marked itself off sharply from the external world and from other people." Every such instance is a "repetition of the same thing" (1919, *S.E.*, XVII: 236).

Freud illustrated with an experience of his own. While in Italy, he unintentionally found himself on a narrow street with "nothing but painted women," peeping from the windows of small houses. He hasted away, only again to find himself on the same street. He scurried away, took a different detour, and again found himself on the same street. There was a sense of helplessness, and of uncanniness[11] (1919, *S.E.*, XVII: 237).

There is thus also the sense of "uncanny" as the involuntary repetition of something inescapable or fateful, which deserves to be spoken of as due to chance. Consider numerical repetition due to chance. There is nothing much uncanny about getting a ticket for one's overcoat with "62" and then finding our room number on a cruise ship to be "62."[12] Yet to come across the number several times in a day is uncanny (1919, *S.E.*, XVII: 237–38).

We arrive at the thesis of *Beyond the Pleasure Principle* (1920), "already completed" while Freud still worked on this 1919 essay.

> It is possible to recognize the dominance in the unconscious mind of a 'compulsion to repeat' proceeding from the instinctual impulses and probably inherent in the very nature of the instincts—a compulsion powerful enough to overrule the pleasure principle, lending to certain aspects of the mind their daemonic character, and still very clearly expressed in the impulses of small children; a compulsion, too, which is responsible for a part of the course taken by the analyses of neurotic patients. (1919, *S.E.*, XVII: 238)

In this passage, it is the compulsion to repeat *unpleasant* experiences—an involuntary repetition and confirmation of destructive impulses—which is perceived to be uncanny. The stage is set for *Beyond the Pleasure Principle.*

Freud then noted that it is a special feature of obsessional neurotics to link events not causally linked. "They are never surprised at their invariably running up against someone they have just been thinking of, perhaps for the first time in a long while." If they mention not having heard from so-and-so for a while, they will invariably receive a letter from the person the next day. They have presentiments that usually come true (1919, *S.E.*, XVII: 239–40).

He attempted to summarize his findings thus far regarding the uncanny. If every effect of an emotional impulse, if repressed, is transformed into anxiety, then there must be a class of frightening things in which "something repressed *recurs*," which constitutes the uncanny. If so, then we can understand the linguistic use of *das Heimliche* as its opposite, *das Unheimliche.* "This uncanny is in reality nothing new or alien, but something which is familiar and old-established in the mind and which has become alienated from it only through the process of repression." It is "something . . . secretly familiar, which has undergone repression and then returned from it" (1919, *S.E.*, XVII: 241 and 245).

One should not be surprised that Freud described a woman's genitals as *unheimlich*. "This *unheimlich* place, however, is the entrance to the former *Heim* [home] of all human beings to the place where each one of us lived once upon a time and in the beginning." And so, when a man—saying to himself, "This place is familiar to me, I've been here before"—suffers from homesickness, he wishes to return to his mother's genitals. Here too the *unheimlich* is what was once *heimlich*, familiar; the prefix "*un*" is the token of repression" (1919, *S.E.*, XVII: 245).

Freud ended with some thoughts concerning "reality-testing." It is noticed that we often slip back to our animistic beliefs, long abandoned, when there is a "mysterious repetition of similar experiences." Yet here there is no appearance of something repressed into consciousness. "What is involved is an actual repression of some content of thought and a return of this repressed content, not a cessation of *belief in the reality* of such a content." Here "repression" is forced. "Animistic beliefs of civilized people are in a state of having been (to a greater or lesser extent) *surmounted*," not repressed. So, the uncanny refers both to a return of repressed material, deemed horrific, and to a time when "primitive beliefs which have been surmounted seem once more to be confirmed" (1919, *S.E.*, XVII: 248–49).

NOTES

1. Zilboorg maintains that the work marks no change of mind for Freud. "What Freud did here was to add a path or two, a little curve or fork, in the tortuous intellectual road which he followed with dogged faith in his own intellectual independence." Gregory Zilboorg, "Introduction, in Sigmund Freud, *Beyond the Pleasure Principle* (New York: W.W. Norton & Company, 1961), xxviii.
2. It is strange that Freud assumes that his translation is the only possible one—"the dream must be interpreted [thus]," given the general unreliability of the method of symbol interpretation.
3. "Dreams are froth."
4. He returns to punishment dreams in chapter 7, where he says punishment dreams are generated by unconscious wishes, but not repressed wishes. "The essential characteristic of punishment dreams would thus be that in their case the dream-constructing wish is not an unconscious wish derived from the repressed (from the system *Ucs.*), but a punitive one reacting against it and belonging to the ego, though at the same time an unconscious (that is to say, preconscious) one" (1900, *S.E.*, IV: 558).
5. In *Interpretation of Dreams*, Freud writes, "[Children] are hard to satisfy, know no such word as 'enough' and insist insatiably on a repetition of things which they have enjoyed or whose taste they liked. It is only the civilizing influence of education that teaches them moderation and how to be content or resigned." It is the same with neurotics (1900, *S.E.*, V: 268n1).
6. A thesis delineated decades later in a brilliant work by philosopher Bernard Suits, in *The Grasshopper*.
7. See Andre Green, "Repetition Compulsion and the Pleasure Principle," http://internationalpsychoanalysis.net/wp-content/uploads/2007/10/greenberlin.pdf, accessed 21 May 2017.
8. Edward Bibring, "The Development and Problems of the Theory of Instincts," *International Journal of Psychoanalysis*, vol. 50, 293–94.
9. Edward Bibring, "The Development and Problems of the Theory of Instincts," 295.

10. Freud is mistaken here, as most of the literature of his day and of days prior links sublimity with dread and horror. Yet he acknowledges his unfamiliarity with that literature at the beginning of this essay (1919, *S.E.*, XVII: 219).

11. One could of course argue that such repetitions were not accidental.

12. The paper was published in 1919. Freud was sixty-two in 1918. It is likely sixty-two was his age at the time of his writing this part of the paper.

Chapter Four

Beyond the Pleasure Principle

Freud's first theory of drives had its roots in Greco-Roman antiquity with the Stoics, who believed upon the birth of any living creature a self-preservative impulse arises, which is also an aversion to anything that might function to destroy it. From a natural impulse of parental affection, there emerged naturally, over time in human beings co-affection and friendship with others. That impulse toward other-concern manifested itself in patriotism, concern for posterity, and even a sense of fit in the cosmos, as well as recommendations on how to live.[1]

A belief in impulses toward self-concern and other-concern was revived in the neo-Stoicism of the Enlightenment and readily found its way thereafter in the early development of the science of psychology. Krafft-Ebing in *Lehrbuch der Psychiatrie* (1890), for instance, wrote of a "drive of self-preservation" (*Erhaltungstrieb*) and a "sex drive" (*Geschlechtstrieb*), the latter being linked to the brain.[2] In "The Aetiology of Hysteria" (1896, *S.E.*, III: 200), Freud posited "the participation of sexual drive forces" (*sexuelle Triebkräfte*) as etiologically indispensable. Two years later in "Sexuality in the Aetiology of Neurosis" (1898, *S.E.*, III: 280–1), he also first mentioned the significance of infantile sexuality as a time where the sexual drive forces are stored to be used later through sublimation. In *Three Essays on the Theory of Sexuality* (1905, *S.E.*, VII: 163 ff.), Freud put forth a sex drive.[3]

The previous chapter among other things told the story of Freud's eventual dissatisfaction with his theory of ego drives and sex drives. By 1920, that dissatisfaction manifested itself in his *Beyond the Pleasure Principle.*

TRAUMATIC NEUROSIS AND CHILDREN'S PLAY

One year after "The Uncanny," Freud attempted a provisional modification of his theory of drives in *Beyond the Pleasure Principle*—a work saturated with metapsychological content. The book marks a major shift in Freud's theoretical thinking. The compulsion to repeat, the driving force of the book, is no longer just an odd phenomenon, characteristic of heightened repression, which signals to an analyst that there is much analytic work to be done. The compulsion to repeat now has metapsychological implications. It is the manifestation of another drive—a death drive (*Todestrieb*). Only with that hypothesis can the problem of traumatic neuroses, with which Freud continually struggled, find apt etiological explanation.

The etiological significance of the compulsion to repeat in Freud's metapsychological frame demands that we give this book due attention. Hence our analysis of this book requires its own chapter.

Freud began, in the first part of the book, with a discussion of the economics of the pleasure principle. Following the lead of G. T. Fechner, human behavior is motivated by an "unpleasurable tension," which finds relief through "avoidance of unpleasure or a production of pleasure." Pleasure (*Lust*) and unpleasure (*Unlust*) relate to "the quantity of excitation that is present in the mind but is not in any way 'bound.'" Pleasure is a diminution of that excitation; unpleasure, an increase. The aim of the system, the principle of constancy, is "to keep the quantity of excitation present in it as low as possible or at least to keep it constant." Only through discussion of this economical factor can he give "the most complete description" of his metapsychology, which involves also topographical and dynamical models (1920, *S.E.*, XVIII: 7–9).

Freud ended the section with two sets of circumstances which work against the principle of constancy. First, there is the maturation of the psychical apparatus, as we see in "Two Principles of Mental Functioning" (1911), where the pleasure principle is "replaced by the reality principle." By demanding of it "postponement of satisfaction, the abandonment of a number of possibilities of gaining satisfaction and the temporary toleration of unpleasure is a step on the long indirect road to pleasure." Second, there is the "release of unpleasure" that occurs as the ego passes into "more highly composite organizations." Certain impulses now prove to be incompatible with other ego-impulses, and so are "split off from this unity by the process of repression, held back at lower levels of psychical development and cut off, to begin with, from the possibility of satisfaction." They seek indirect routes or substitutive satisfactions which are experienced by the ego as unpleasant (1920, *S.E.*, XVIII: 10–11).

Such concerns, however, are merely prefatory. The second section is an investigation of a deep substantive problem, to which we have already been introduced: traumatic neurosis. Traumatic neurosis is akin to hysteria in that it has many similar efferent symptoms, but differs from it in "its strongly marked signs of subjective ailment," characterized by greater enfeeblement of and disturbances in mentation. Traumatic neurosis has been among Freud's enigmata over the decades, as "no complete explanation has yet been reached either of war neuroses or of the traumatic neuroses of peace" (1920, *S.E.*, XVIII: 12).

Enter dreams, the study of which "may be considered the most trustworthy method of investigating deep mental processes," and repetition. He states, "Dreams occurring in traumatic neuroses have the characteristic of repeatedly bringing the patient back into the situation of his accident, a situation from which he wakes up in another fright." That shows a fixation to the trauma and suggests treatment of the cathartic sort Freud and Breuer proffered in 1895 (1920, *S.E.*, XVIII: 13).

There is no evidence, and this claim would now be viewed with incredulity, that those suffering from traumatic neuroses are much occupied in waking life by their trauma—thereby suggesting that the trauma is nowise experienced as pleasant. If dreams are expressions of a wish fulfilllment, then it would be strange that such recurrent dreams repeatedly take back sufferers to their trauma. Freud was left to conclude either that such dreams are not wish fulfilllment or that the ego is masochistic. Concluding that in traumatic dreams, the function of dreaming is "diverted from its purposes," he is left to explore the "mysterious masochistic trends of the ego" (1920, *S.E.*, XVIII: 13–14).

Freud next returned to the topic of children's playing, which we covered in chapter 3, when we examined *Jokes and their Relation to the Unconscious* and his essay "Creative Writers and Day-Dreaming." He scrutinized a class of repetitive behavior of his own grandson, Ernst Halberstadt, at one and a half years of age. The child, though not in the least precocious, was a good, well-behaved boy, who was much attached to his mother, the child's chief caregiver. Freud noticed that the child never cried when his mother would leave him for a few hours (1920, *S.E.*, XVIII: 14).

Ernst, fond of throwing away toys and hunting after them, stumbled upon a new game, which he constantly repeated. One day, he tossed a wooden reel with attached string behind a curtained cot, where it disappeared from view, though the string did not. He then made the reel reappear by pulling the string. With its reemergence, he exclaimed, *da* ("there") and repeated the activity tirelessly, with the same verbal *da* each time. Freud interpreted the repetitive behavior of the boy. "The interpretation of the game . . . was related to the child's great cultural achievement—the instinctual renunciation . . . which he had made in allowing his mother to go away without protesting." In short, *tossing the stick = reliving of the pain he felt when his mother would leave him,*

and

retrieving the stick by pulling the string = his joy upon her return.

"As a rule one only witnessed its first act, which was repeated untiringly as a game in itself, thought there is no doubt that the greater pleasure was attached to the second act" (1920, *S.E.*, XVIII: 15–16).

What stood out for Freud was that the repetitive behavior in which the boy was untiringly engaged had a most unpleasant element—his mother's departure. "How then," said Freud, "does his repetition of this distressing experience as a game fit in with the pleasure principle?" One answer is the unpleasant first part of the game, her departure, was suffered so that the pleasant second part of the game, her return, could be enjoyed. Against that view of the matter, there is the observation that Ernst engaged in the first part of the game without the second far more often than the game as a whole—which suggests a masochistic tendency of the child (1920, *S.E.*, XVIII: 15–16).

Freud offered two interpretations. First, the child could have been behaving in pursuance of an impulse for mastery, independent of the pleasure/unpleasure of the situation. "He was in a *passive* situation—he was overpowered by the experience; but, by repeating it, unpleasurable though it was, as a game, he took on an *active* part." Second, the child could have been behaving in pursuance of an impulse for vengeance. "All right, then, go away! I don't need you. I'm sending you away myself."[4] Freud was left to ponder whether Ernst's behavior, seemingly incongruent with the pleasure principle, is evidence of another drive which attempts to master overpowering experiences—an independent, primitive principle, with its own energy—something beyond the pleasure principle. "The child may, after all, only have been able to repeat his unpleasant experience in play because the repetition carried along with it a yield of pleasure of another sort but none the less a direct one"—the pleasure of mastery or of revenge (1920, *S.E.*, XVIII: 16).

It will, added Freud, not do to note that "children repeat everything that has make a great impression on them in real life." One wishes to know why unpleasant experiences find their way into play. If a child experiences unpleasantly a doctor probing down his throat, he will certainly do the same with a playmate, "and in this way revenges himself on a substitute." Moreover, consider artistic play and imitation. In tragedy, for instance, the most pain-filled experiences are at once extraordinarily enjoyable (1920, *S.E.*, XVIII: 16–17).

Such things noted, it does seem that there is the possibility of accommodating Ernst's traumatic experience, even those of soldiers', with the pleasure principle, yet Freud is unwilling to do just that (1920, *S.E.*, XVIII: 17).

BEYOND THE TOPOGRAPHICAL MODEL

Freud began the third section with a summary of the development of psychoanalytic technique over time. First, a therapist did nothing but discover unconscious material and communicate it to a patient. That was cathartic, not curative. Next, there came the step of an analyst forming a construction, through overcoming resistances, to be confirmed by the patient—that is, "suggestion operating as 'transference.'" That failed to make conscious all that was unconscious. Third, to get at the essential part of what remains unconscious, a patient was "obliged to *repeat* the repressed material as a contemporary experience instead of . . . *remembering* it as something belonging to the past"—in other words, a compulsion to repeat. With this technique the prior neurosis is supplanted by a transference neurosis, with the aim of the analyst being to "force as much as possible into the channel of memory and to allow as little as possible to emerge as repetition." The ultimate end is to show the patient that what seems to have been reality is merely a "reflection of a forgotten past" (1920, *S.E.*, XVIII: 18–19).

Here Freud noted limits to the "purely descriptive" topographical model of *The Interpretation of Dreams*. It is unavailing to speak of the unconscious as the resisting force, as what is unconscious aims to "break through the pressure weighing down on it." Thus, we must introduce additional terminology. A more serviceable distinction is between "the coherent *ego* and the *repressed*," as much of the ego is repressed, while only a small part is preconscious. Now "the patient's resistance arises from his ego, and we then at once perceive that the compulsion to repeat must be ascribed to the unconscious repressed," and can manifest itself only after treatment "has gone halfway to meet it and has loosened the repression" (1920, *S.E.*, XVIII: 19–20). Freud now is working toward the "systemic or dynamic" structural model he will move to in three years and which will play large in group-psychology works such as *Civilization and Its Discontents*.

Freud acknowledged that resistance of the conscious and unconscious ego works in pursuance of the pleasure principle. The difficulty is a patient's tolerance of unpleasure (*Unlust*) by appealing to the reality principle. "How is the compulsion to repeat—the manifestation of the power of the repressed—related to the pleasure principle?" Most of what is reexperienced through the compulsion to repeat must be unpleasant, as it brings to light "activities of repressed instinctual impulses."—such as recognition of sibling hatred. Still nothing here is inconsistent with the pleasure principle, as "unpleasure for one system [is] simultaneously satisfaction for the other." Yet Freud clung to the sentiment that something is awry: There is something in such compulsive behaviors beyond the pleasure principle. Freud claimed he had discovered a novelty. "We come now to a new and remarkable fact, namely that the compulsion to repeat also recalls from the past experiences which include no possibility of pleasure, and which can never, even long ago, have brought satisfaction even to instinctual impulses which have since been repressed" (1920, *S.E.*, XVIII: 19–20).

The issue is not so much active, but passive, experiences. "This 'perpetual recurrence of the same thing' causes us no astonishment when it relates to *active* behavior on the part of the person concerned and when we can discern in him an essential character-trait which always remains the same and which is compelled to find expression in a repetition of the same experiences. We are much more impressed by cases where the subject appears to have a *passive* experience, over which he has no influence, but in which he meets with a repetition of the same fatality" (1920, *S.E.*, XVIII: 21–22). These kinds of passive experiences imply something independent of the pleasure principle.

Freud offered actual and fictive observations as examples. First there is the play of children, which seems to answer both to the pleasure principle and the daemonic compulsion to repeat. By acting out "dangerous" situations, they gain mastery of powerful impressions—a source of pleasure—and "they are inexorable in their insistence that the repetition shall be an identical one."[5] Next, there was a female who married three times and each time her husband fell ill and had to be nursed by her as he lay dying. Last, he cites the fictive hero Tancred, of Tasso's *Gerusalemme Liberata.* The hero tragically not only kills his beloved Clorinda, disguised as an enemy, in a duel, but also, upon entering a magic forest, he slashes a tree, only to see blood gush from it, and he thereby hears again Clorinda's voice. He has again injured her (1920, *S.E.*, XVIII: 22 and 35).

Freud stated, "If we take into account observations such as these, based upon behavior in the transference and upon the life-histories of men and women, we shall find courage to assume that there really does exist in the mind a compulsion to repeat which overrides the pleasure principle." Yet that compulsion rarely occurs "unsupported by other motives," in keeping with the pleasure principle. That compulsion is manifest with least dilution in the dreams of traumatic neurotics, but also in the phenomenon of transference and in the play of children, which we have seen also answers in part to the pleasure principle (1920, *S.E.*, XVIII: 23).

THE CONSERVATIVE NATURE OF DRIVES

In the fourth section—a brilliant metapsychological section—Freud started a detailed metapsychological excursion with the aim of explication of his enigma: traumatic neurosis. The system *Cs.* (consciousness) carries no bound energy, but only energy capable of free discharge. It is also shielded from external stimulation by a protective shield, which is "an almost more important function for the living organism than *reception* of stimuli." The system receives stimuli "in small specimens" to "discover the direction and nature of the sternal stimuli." In complex organisms, the receptive cortical layer is withdrawn and has left portions, the sensory organs, as sensory receptors to take in small samples of external stimulation (1920, *S.E.*, XVIII: 27–28).

The system *Cs.* conforms to the pleasure principle and is shielded from excessive stimulation from outside by its protective shield, but there is no such shield from internal excitations. When internal excitations become too intense and lead to increase of unpleasure, the system treats them as if they had come from the external world—hence, projection (1920, *S.E.*, XVIII: 28–29).

Freud was then readied to tackle cases prima facie inconsistent with "the dominance of the pleasure principle." He returned to traumatic neurosis. "We describe as 'traumatic' any excitations from outside which are powerful enough to break through the protective shield." Once done, the system takes every possible defensive posture. Yet so disturbed is the system that it cannot shield itself from excessive stimuli. To protect the system, "cathected energy is summoned from all sides to provide sufficiently high cathexes of energy in the environs of the breach. An 'anticathexis' on a grand scale is set up, for whose benefit all the other psychical systems are impoverished, so that the remaining psychical functions are extensively paralysed or reduced." Mechanical violence to the system is a source of sexual agitation which leads to the traumatic effect. Resistance to the flood of excitations is determined by readiness of the system: a high-cathected system being ever ready to bind inflowing excitations (1920, *S.E.*, XVIII: 29–33). A picture readily forms of the frantic defensive postures assumed with a break in the phalanx of a defending army, whose king is now exposed to the enemy.

Freud was then positioned to explain the dreams of those suffering from traumatic neurosis. The usual function of dreaming is to fulfill wishes in a hallucinatory manner and in keeping with the pleasure principle. However, that clearly is not the case in recurrent nightmares of traumatic neurotics. "We may assume . . . that dreams are here helping to carry out another task, which must be accomplished before the dominance of the pleasure principle can even begin. These dreams are endeavouring to master the stimulus retrospectively, by developing the anxiety whose omission was the cause of the traumatic neurosis." Yet here we have a peek at a principle independent of the pleasure principle and "more primitive than the purpose of gaining pleasure and avoiding pain" (1920, *S.E.*, XVIII: 31–32).

Thus there must be a revision to the theory of dreams as wish-fulfillments. Anxiety and punishment dreams are unproblematic, as they fulfill the "wish of the sense of guilt." Nonetheless, "it is impossible to classify as wish-fulfilllments the dreams we have been discussing which occur in traumatic neuroses, or the dream during psycho-analyses which bring to memory the psychical traumas of childhood. They arise, rather, in obedience to the compulsion to repeat." This "beyond the pleasure principle" implies a "time before the purpose of dreams was the fulfilllment of wishes" and points to such dreams occurring "*outside* analysis" (1920, *S.E.*, XVIII: 32–33).

In patients compulsively repeating events in analysis, transference shows disregard for the pleasure principle, as "the repressed memory-traces of his primaeval experiences are not present in him in a bound state," thus they are incapable of obeying the demands of the secondary process (i.e., the ego). Not being bound, they freely find their way into dreams. The compulsion to repeat also shows itself in the transference relationship with an analyst—a patient's unwillingness to detach himself from his analyst. Last, feelings of dread are instances of the compulsion—a "hint of possession by some 'daemonic' power" (1920, *S.E.*, XVIII: 36). Thus traumatic dreams, transference, and dread indicate something fundamental—a daemonic human drive.

"We have come upon the track of a universal attribute of instincts and perhaps of organic life in general," stated Freud. "*It seems, then, that an instinct is an urge inherent in organic life to restore an earlier state of things* which the living entity has been obliged to abandon under the pressure of external disturbing forces; that is, it is a kind of organic elasticity, or, to put it another way, the expression of the inertia inherent in organic life." Consider other organisms. Some fishes return to their spawning grounds at spawning time to drop their eggs. It is the same with flights of migratory birds. He again appealed to recapitulationism. "The germ of every living animal is obliged in the course of its development to recapitulate (even if only in a transient and abbreviated fashion) the structures of all the forms from which it is sprung, instead of proceeding quickly by the shortest path to its final shape." Many animals, having lost an organ, regenerate another identical one. According to Freud, "All the organic instincts are conservative, are acquired historically and tend towards the restoration of an earlier state of things" (1920, *S.E.*, XVIII: 36–38)—that is, fundamentally drives of repetition.

Given the provisionally accepted definition, it follows that living entities, as repetitive entities and with such repetitions aiming at identity of repetition, have no wish to change, indeed are change resistant, as the principle of constancy would imply. In a stable milieu, each would "constantly repeat the same course of life." Thus it is changes on the earth that force changes in an organism's course of life. "Every modification which is thus imposed upon the course of an organism's life is accepted by the conservative organic instincts and stored up for further repetition. Those instincts are therefore bound to give a deceptive appearance of being forces tending towards change and progress, whilst in fact they are merely seeking to reach an ancient goal by paths alike old and new." Consequently, there is an aim to all organic striving and that aim, consistent with the conservative nature of drives, cannot be something alien. "It must be an *old* state of things, an initial state from which the living entity has at one time or other departed and to which it is striving to return by the circuitous paths along which its development leads." Here we arrive at life's fundamental repetition, thus expressible: "everything living dies for *internal* reasons," "*the aim of life is death*," or "*inanimate things existed before living ones*" (1920, *S.E.*, XVIII: 38).

The first organisms, speculated Freud, were short-lived, as the change from inanimate to animate matter had to have created the first drive—the drive to "cancel itself out" and "return to the inanimate state." Environmental changes forced changes, "complicated *détours*," to the simple organic structures that delayed onset of death (1920, *S.E.*, XVIII: 38–39).

What then of the self-preservative drives? "They are component instincts whose function is to assure that the organism shall follow its own path to death, and to ward off any possible ways of returning to inorganic existence other than those which are immanent in the organism itself"—in other words, "the organism wishes to die only in its own fashion." He summed up poetically, "Thus these guardians of life, too, were originally the myrmidons of death." In this manner, we find an explanation of humans' struggles against perceived dangers (1920, *S.E.*, XVIII: 39).

What of human sexuality? Early germ cells, with "inherited and freshly acquired instinctual dispositions," retained the original structure of living matter and separated themselves from organisms. In favorable circumstances, they develop—that is, "they repeat the performance to which they owe their existence." He added, "This function of the germ cell is reinforced, or only made possible, if it coalescence with another cell similar to itself and yet differing from it." Thus, there comes to be a group of drives which guard the whole organism, that offer them shelter from the stimuli of the external world, and that bring about coalescence with other germ cells—the sexual drives. They are conservative (repetitive) in that they "bring back earlier states of living substances," "they are peculiarly resistant to eternal influences," and "they preserve life." In doing so, "they operate against the purpose of the other instincts, which leads, by reason of their function, to death." While the death instincts rush forth "to reach the final aim of life as swiftly as possible," the sexual instincts jerk back "to make a fresh start and so prolong the journey" (1920, *S.E.*, XVIII: 40–41).

So, with the beginnings of life, sexuality did not exist, though the sexual drives "may have been in operation from the very first," and only later they began to function in opposing the work of the ego drives, which "exercise pressure towards death" (1920, *S.E.*, XVIII: 41–44).

Freud again appealed to biology to buttress his new theory of drives. According to Weismann, a living body has mortal and immortal parts. The body, narrowly construed in a nonsexual (nonreproductive) manner, is subject to death. The germ cells, in contrast, can live forever insofar as, under favorable conditions, they are able "to surround themselves with a new body." Thus, germ cells, concerned with reproduction, function for the survival of a species. Freud, offering "a dynamic corollary to Weismann's morphological theory" but concerning himself with "the forces operating on [the body]" and not the body, posits a drive that leads what is living to death and another which is "perpetually attempting and achieving a renewal of life" (1920, *S.E.*, XVIII: 45–46).

Yet Weismann's account was of multi-celled organisms. According to Weismann, the picture differed for single-celled organisms, which seemingly live forever, as each such organism, once mature, reproduces through division—eternality through repetition. Freud himself referred to observations by the biologist Woodruff, who observed a ciliate infusorian which reproduced through division into the 3,019th generation, at which point Woodruff stopped observations. Others have shown, pace Woodruff, that there is a point in those divisions in which infusoria become enfeebled and diminished in size, without recuperative measures (1920, *S.E.*, XVIII: 47–48).

What did Freud take from those observations? It is the notion of a natural death, even for single cell organisms.

There are, however, recuperative measures—"certain stimulating agents" like altering the fluid in which they find nutriment—one of which is of utmost significance. If any two infusoria prior to the point of senescence, are able to commingle, "they are saved from growing old and become 'rejuvinated.'" Freud adds, "Conjugation is no doubt the fore-runner of the sexual reproduction of higher creatures; it is as yet unconnected with propagation and is limited to the mixing of the substances of the two individuals" (1920, *S.E.*, XVIII: 48).

Still, even infusoria likely "die a natural death as a result of their own vital processes." Woodruff was able to observe reproduction of infusoria for so many generations only because he gave each generation fresh nutrient fluid, otherwise he noted that the infusoria "were injured by the products of metabolism which they extruded into the surrounding fluid." That for Freud showed that "it was only the products of its *own* metabolism which had fatal results for the particular kind of animalcule. For the same animalculae, which inevitably perished if they were crowded together in their own nutrient fluid, flourished in a solution which was over-saturated with the waste products of a distantly related species"[6] (1920, *S.E.*, XVIII: 48).

Do not such observations prove troublesome for a death drive, seeking to return the organic to the inorganic?

No, claimed Freud. What seems immortal, the infusoria, cannot be separated from the mortal bodies in which they exist. Moreover, a death drive might still be operative in such simple organisms, "yet their effects may be so completely concealed by the life-preserving forces that it may be very hard to find any direct evidence of their presence." If so, "The striking similarity between Weismann's distinction of soma and germ-plasm and our separation of the death instincts from the life instincts persists and retains its significance"[7] (1920, *S.E.*, XVIII: 49). The possible "solution" is more ad hoc than plausible.

Freud then extrapolated from microbiology to psychoanalysis. The life drives, active in each cell, take other cells as their object, and in such a manner they "partly neutralize the death instincts." Thus, "the germ cells require their libido, the activity of their life instincts, for themselves, as a reserve against their later momentous constructive activity." Here we coalesce with the findings of poets and philosophers who have posited that Eros is the binding force of all living things (1920, *S.E.*, XVIII: 50).

Freud then turned to a brief history of his theory of drives, motivated by the problem of the transference neuroses. Psychoanalysis began by acceptance of the traditional distinction between drives of hunger (ego: individual-preserving) and love (sexual: species-preserving), and was able to understand much of psychoneurosis. Still, the sex drive in, for instance, the transference neuroses, was "extended so as to cover many things which could not be classed under the reproductive function" (1920, *S.E.*, XVIII: 51–52).

Step 2 was to go beyond the notion of ego as a censoring agency, "capable of erecting protective structures and reactive formations." There came inversion—the phenomenon in which libido is withdrawn from objects and directed to the ego, which results in "narcissism."[8] This drive account of narcissism left the distinction between ego drives and sexual drives, each with its own drive-energy, without a motivation. There was merely a certain drive-energy, libido, which could be attached to objects or the ego. "The distinction between the two kinds of instinct, which was originally regarded as in some sort of way *qualitative*, must now be characterized differently—namely as being *topographical*. Thus, the transference neuroses "are the result of a conflict between the ego and the libidinal cathexis of objects" (1920, *S.E.*, XVIII: 52–53).

Step 3 is recognition that the self-preservative drives are libidinal. "We are venturing upon the further step of recognizing the sexual instinct as Eros, the preserve of all things, and of deriving the narcissistic libido of the ego from the stores of libido by means of which the cells of the soma are attached to one another" (1920, *S.E.*, XVIII: 52).

Is there then only one drive and one form of drive-energy, libido? Freud attempted to answer that question by giving arguments, or at least considerations, for a death drive.

First, there is the problem of pansexualism. If we limit ourselves to one drive, "we shall after all be driven to agree with the critics who suspected from the first that psycho-analysis explains *everything* by sexuality." Psychoanalysis can escape that criticism by positing a drive in opposition to the sexual drive (1920, *S.E.*, XVIII: 52).

Thus we must (step 4) go beyond the pleasure principle. Freud consolidated his dualism. "Our views have from the very first been *dualistic*, and today they are even more definitely dualistic than before—now that we describe the opposition as being, not between ego-instincts and sexual instincts but between life instincts and death instincts" (1920, *S.E.*, XVIII: 52–53).

Second, there is the problem of hate, which formerly was explained by there being a sadistic component in the sexual drive. "How can the sadistic instinct, whose aim it is to injure the object, be derived from Eros, the preserver of life? Is it not plausible to suppose that this sadism is in fact a death instinct which, under the influence of the narcissistic libido, has been forced away from the ego and has consequently only emerged in relation to the object?" Doing so, it served the sexual function (1920, *S.E.*, XVIII: 53–54).

Freud thus took himself to have a "better" explanation of sadism and masochism in sexuality. Sadism begins in orality, where "erotic mastery over an object coincides with that object's destruction." The sadistic impulse later separates itself from its libidinal function, and during the genital stage, the sadistic impulse takes on the task of overpowering the sexual object for the sake of reproduction—hence, love and hate in erotic life. Masochism, hitherto explained as sadism turned toward the ego, can now be explained as a regression to "an earlier phase of the instinct's history." Moreover, the door is left open for the existence of primary masochism (1920, *S.E.*, XVIII: 54).

The account is counterintuitive, as it makes every "normal" sexual act an act of violence and hatred, though the conclusion can be made more appetizing by granting that the proportions of love, violence, and hate may differ between types of sexual acts. Freud acknowledged the difficulty, as he said the impression is "positively mystical." "It looks suspiciously as though we were trying to find a way out of a highly embarrassing situation at any price" (1920, *S.E.*, XVIII: 54).

REPEATEDLY COMBINING FACTS WITH SPECULATION

Freud returned to germ cells and sexual reproduction. He noticed a problem. "We cannot ascribe to the sexual instinct the characteristic of a compulsion to repeat," which is what led us to the death drive. "The sphere of embryonic developmental processes is no doubt extremely rich in such phenomena of repetition; the two germ cells that are involved in sexual reproduction and their life history are themselves only repetitions of the beginnings of organic life." Yet sexual life aims at "the coalescence of two cell-bodies" (1920, *S.E.*, XVIII: 56), so there is more work to do on the issue.

Following Darwin, at some point in evolution, there came about by chance the conjugation of two Protista and that conjugation was found to be advantageous, so it was "retained and further exploited." "On this view 'sex' would not be anything very ancient; and the extraordinary violent instincts whose aim it is to bring about sexual union would be repeating something that had once occurred by chance and had since become established as being advantageous" (1920, *S.E.*, XVIII:56–57).

There is a difficulty. Why would there be retention and further exploitation, for example showing that they do not lower an organism's fitness? Do they not presuppose a binding impulse—a sexual impulse? So, it seems, we must assume the existence of a sexual drive with a death drive. Still, "in that case we shall be working on an equation with two unknown quantities" (1920, *S.E.*, XVIII: 57).

Here we segue to the realm of myth and away from biological science. Freud rehashed briefly the account of human sexuality given by Aristophanes in Plato's *Symposium*. Aristophanes thought that humans were originally round and of three sorts: male, female, and androgynous. Each had two faces (opposed), two sets of arms and legs, and two genitalia (opposed). They had angered Zeus, and the king of gods punished them through halving each. Human halves, thereafter, would be involved in an amaranthine struggle to find their other half to again make them whole. Might it not be the same with living substances? (1920, *S.E.*, XVIII: 57–58).

Freud acknowledged that the mythic account and indeed his own were phantasmagoric. He was unsure whether he himself believed what he had written. Might not he have overestimated the significance of the compulsion to repeat? He admitted falling back on another repetition of a sort. "It is impossible to pursue an idea of this kind except by repeatedly combining factual material with what is purely speculative and thus diverging widely from empirical observation." Of course, the more speculation there is, the greater "the degree of uncertainty," though there may be a "lucky hit." Moreover, impartiality is scientifically impossible when one considers "the great problems of science and life." He consoled himself. "It is surely possible to throw oneself into a line of thought and to follow it wherever it leads out of simple scientific curiosity, or . . . as an *advocatus diaboli*, who is not on that account himself sold to the devil" (1920, *S.E.*, XVIII: 59).

There are two other problems: the problem of metapsychological language and the problem of borrowing from biology. First, the metapsychological language employed throughout gives the impression of there being more nonsense than science in these hypotheses. There is talk about one drive casting off another or a drive turning from the ego to an object. That is because Freud is "obliged to operate with the scientific terms . . . or the figurative language, peculiar to psychology"—the language of depth psychology. Such difficulties would dissolve if the psychological terms could be supplanted by physio-chemical ones, but they too are part of another figurative language, but one that is more familiar to readers. Second, by drawing so much from biology to speculate on metapsychological explanation, Freud falls prey to objections concerning dubious analogical reasoning and extrapolations. What is true biologically may not be true psychologically.[9] Still, if anything is unsure, it is the psychology, not the biology, even though it was the clinical material about narcissism that drove his posit and led to Freud rummaging through biology for further support of it. The findings in that rich science in a short time "may be of a kind which will blow away the whole of our artificial structure of hypotheses" (1920, *S.E.*, XVIII: 60).

In the final section of the book, Freud reviewed his speculative "findings." "The pleasure principle, then, is a tendency operating in the service of a function whose business it is to free the mental apparatus entirely from excitation or to keep the amount of excitation in it constant or to keep it as low as possible." Yet the most universal endeavor of a living substance [is] to return to the quiescence of the inorganic world." As the sexual act allows for a "momentary extinction of a highly intensified excitation," so too is "the binding of an instinctual impulse . . . a preliminary function designed to prepare the excitation for its final elimination in the pleasure of discharge"—that is, the eternal extinction of the organism (1920, *S.E.*, XVIII: 62).

Concerning the excitatory paths of Eros and the death drives, Freud believed for a variety of reasons that the death drive does its work unobtrusively—that is, it is an unbound excitatory process—while Eros, "constantly producing tensions whose release is felt as pleasure," chiefly by binding excitations (1920, *S.E.*, XVIII: 77).

UPSHOT

In "Remembering, Repeating, and Working-Through" (1914), the compulsion to repeat was a clinical concept. Six years later, it becomes a metapsychological construct, a transformation that is outlined in nine steps by Nicole Kirman.[10]

1. The compulsion to repeat "is now defined as a tendency to repeat 'unpleasurable' experiences."
2. The compulsion to repeat has become a regulatory principle on par with the pleasure principle.
3. The compulsion to repeat is characteristic of the repressed unconscious.
4. The compulsion to repeat is characteristic of all drives inasmuch as it is conservative.
5. The compulsion to repeat is a retrograde force.
6. The compulsion to repeat at times regulates the death drive and at other times is "the 'visible' manifestation of [its] 'silent' work."
7. The compulsion to repeat "serves to restore 'pretraumatic' conditions" by binding building energy when the pleasure principle is inoperable and by creating the anxiety that was missing when the trauma occurred.
8. The compulsion to repeat allows for active mastery of the traumatic scenario.
9. The compulsion to repeat "is an essential part of the process of abreaction."

Was Freud, with his commitment to a theory of drives, right to subsume the ego drives and sex drives under Eros and adopt the notion of a death drive, on indecisive evidence of a daemonic compulsion to repeat? We delay answer to that question to chapter 6.

NOTES

1. M. Andrew Holowchak, *The Stoics: A Guide for the Perplexed* (London: Continuum Books, 2008), 36–37.

2. Richard von Krafft-Ebing in *Lehrbuch der Psychiatrie* (Stuttgart: Ferdinand Enke, 1890), 87–88.

3. For a fine account of *Trieb*, *Impuls*, *Drang*, and *Instinkt* among anthropologists, physiologists, and psychiatrists prior to 1900 and of the development of Freud's early thinking on drives, see Patricia Cotti, "Freud and the Sexual Drive before 1905: From Hesitation to Adoption," *History of the Human Sciences*, vol. 21, no. 3, 2008, 26–44.

4. Freud notes that one year later, Ernst would take toys at which he was angry and toss them to the floor and exclaim, "Go to the front!" At the time, his father, Freud's son, was at the front and the child was making best use of his sole possession of his mother" (1920, *S.E.*, XVIII: 16).

5. It is the same with stories told to children. "Children never tire of asking an adult to repeat a game what he has shown them or played with them, till he is too exhausted to go on. And if a child has been told a nice story, he will insist on hearing it over and over again rather than a new one and he will remorselessly stipulate that the repetition shall be an identical on

and will correct any alterations of which the narrator may be guilty." He adds, "None of this contradicts the pleasure principle; repetition, the re-experiencing of something identical, is clearly in itself a source of pleasure (1920, *S.E.*, XVIII: 35–36).

6. It is natural to form a picture of a similar fate for humans, overpopulating the globe, depleting and contaminating resources, and suffering self-annihilation.

7. Freud notes that he has unwittingly steered his course "into the harbor of Schopenhauer's philosophy" (1920, *S.E.*, XVIII: 49–50).

8. Freud incautiously concludes here, "The ego is the true and original reservoir of libido"—a statement which he amends in *The Ego and the Id*, where the id is the libidinal reservoir.

9. Bocock goes too far. "Data from biology cannot be used to justify theoretical change within a different science." R. J. Bocock, "Freud and the Centrality of Instincts in Psychoanalytic Sociology," *British Journal of Sociology*, vol. 28, no. 4, 1977, 474.

10. Nicole F. Kirman, "The Repetition Compulsion Revisited," *Issues in Psychoanalytic Psychology*," vol. 18, no. 1, 1996, 36–37.

Chapter Five

Compulsion to Repeat and the Death Drive in Later Works

Freud's *Beyond the Pleasure Principle* was a landmark work in psychoanalysis. In it, Freud dealt with what he took to be observational challenges to this theory of drives: the problem of narcissism and certain masochistic tendencies in the play of children as well as punishment dreams. Such observations pointed to the inadequacy of his theory of drives, and so he posited, if only tentatively, a drive that aims at annihilation. He iterated the posit three years later in *The Ego and the Id*, another book rich in metapsychological content.

In this chapter, we focus on the death drive as it plays out after *Beyond the Pleasure Principle.* We examine three works: *The Ego and the Id*, *Civilization and Its Discontents*, and a 1932 essay on war.

ADOPTION OF THE DEATH DRIVE

The year 1923 for Freud was another turning point. In *The Ego and the Id*, he came to terms with two shortcomings. First, acknowledging the limits of his topographical model (the systems *Cs.*, *Pcs.*, and *Ucs.*)—the system *Pcs.* is unsuitable as the censoring agency for dreams (1900, *S.E.*, IV: 567–68) and consciousness, the part of the system of which we are directly aware, "is in no way suited to serve as a criterion for the differentiation of systems"[1] (1915, *S.E.*, XIV: 192)—he explained and defended his structural model (id, ego, and superego). Moreover and more relevantly for this undertaking, Freud announced the death drive as part of his psychoanalytic thinking.

"I have lately developed a view of the instincts which I shall here hold and take as the basis of my further discussion."[2] The first group, under Eros, "is by far the most conspicuous and accessible to study." In Eros, we have the uninhibited sexual instinct proper as well as aim-inhibited or sublimated impulses and the ego- or self-preservative drive. The anabolic Eros, by "bringing about a more and more far-reaching combination of the particles into which living substance is dispersed," aims at complicating and preserving life. The second group, comprising the death drives, is discernible by its sadism. The catabolic death drive aims to take what was once inorganic and return it to that state. Thus both drives are conservative (repetitive) in that each "would be endeavouring to re-establish a state of things that was disturbed by the emergence of life." How is that so? "The emergence of life would thus be the cause of the continuance of life and also at the same time of the striving towards death; and life itself would be a conflict and compromise between these two trends" (1923, *S.E.*, XIX: 40–41). In such a manner, there is a substantive, though biological, answer to the question: What is the meaning of life?

"Every particle of living substance," Freud stated, contains something of each drive, though in unbalanced proportions. That is, of course, a wild hypothesis, and Freud can offer no sure account of how the two are "alloyed" or "fused" in each living particle, but it is "an assumption indispensable to our conception" (1923, *S.E.*, XIX: 41), a common argument to justify a claim: its utility.

Drawing abundantly from his understanding of biological data that he believed supported his speculations in *Beyond the Pleasure Principle*, he continued on the process of erotic fusion. In the process of unicellular organisms combining to form multicellular organisms, "the death instinct of the single cell can successfully be neutralized and the destructive impulses be diverted on to the external world through the instrumentality of a special organ"—the muscular apparatus—which then can act destructively against other organisms and the external world (1923, *S.E.*, XIX: 41).

Against this process of erotic fusion, there must also be working a process of destructive defusion. "For the purposes of discharge the instinct of destruction is habitually brought into the service of Eros" for defusion. The destructive drive occurs in epileptic fits and obsessional neuroses. "Making a swift generalization, we might conjecture that the essence of regression of libido (e.g., from the genital to the sadistic-anal phase) lies in a defusion of instincts, just as, conversely, the advance from the earlier phase to the definitive genital one would be conditioned by a accession of erotic components." It might be the same with the "fundamental phenomenon" of ambivalence, though Freud settled on the likelihood that it is failed fusion (1923, *S.E.*, XIX: 41–42).

The hypothesis, now posited with the supplementation of biological evidence, is whether there is additional psychological evidence of the clinical sort to confirm the distinction? He had already, as noted above, claimed justification based on its ability to provide a better account of the totality of clinical facts.

At this juncture of the argument, ambivalence, a fundamental clinical concept, comes into play. Clinical observation shows a dispositional shift from love to hate and from hate to love with "unexpected regularity." "If this change is more than a mere succession in time—if, that is, one of them actually turns into the other—then clearly the ground is cut away from under a distinction so fundamental as that between erotic instincts and death instincts, one which presupposes physiological processes running in opposite directions." Consider persecutory paranoia. In this disorder, as Freud then understood it, someone fending off homosexual feelings transfers feelings of love into hate. The loved one becomes a persecutor, "against whom the patient directs an often dangerous aggressiveness." Moreover, hostility often leads to homosexual attachment. Why? "The hostile attitude has no prospect of satisfaction," so for economic reasons it is supplanted by love. Are we to assume in such cases a direct transformation? (1923, *S.E.*, XIX: 42–44).

Clinical observation suggests otherwise. "An ambivalent attitude is present from the outset and the transformation is effected by means of a reactive displacement of cathexis, energy being withdrawn from the erotic impulses and added to the hostile one." Yet that scenario presupposes a neutral "displaceable energy," which can be used for the purpose of binding destruction and which is active in the id and the ego, and which is sexualized Eros of the narcissistic sort. That shows the erotic drives "are more plastic, more readily diverted and displaced than the destructive instincts." Once again, Freud appeals to theoretical indispensability. "Without assuming the existence of a displaceable energy of this kind we can make no headway." He add, "I am only putting forth a hypothesis; I have no proof to offer" (1923, *S.E.*, XIX: 44–45).

There does seem to be clinical support for that hypothesis. There are the "cathectic processes of the id," in which "there is peculiar indifference in regard to the object," and transference in the analytic setting.[3] And so, this desexualized energy can be described as "*sublimated* energy," which can go to the unifying aims of the ego, which also involve thought processes. Hence we arrive at a possible explanation of the mechanism of sublimation. We also have a possible explanation of identification, in which erotic aims are frustrated on account of the ego—erotic libido being transformed into ego libido. In such a manner, "the ego is working in opposition to the purposes of Eros and working at the service of the opposing instinctual impulses"—the death drives. Finally, we also have a possible explanation of narcissism. At first, all libido is in the id, but as a human matures, some of the libido goes out to others. The mature ego then tries to "force itself on the id as a love-object" (1923, *S.E.*, XIX: 45–46). However, these explanation do not dovetail well into Freud's subsequent discovery of signal anxiety that he described in 1926.

"Over and over again we find," said Freud, "when we are able to trace instinctual impulses back, that they reveal themselves as derivatives of Eros." Were it not for the sadistic observations in *Beyond the Pleasure Principle*, he added, "We should have difficulty in holding to our fundamental dualistic point of view. But since we cannot escape that view, we are driven to conclude that the death instincts are by their nature mute and that the clamour of life proceeds for the most part from Eros" (1923, *S.E.*, XIX: 46).

At this point, readers will sense great tension, and a certain bit of frustration at the theoretical complexity. If the death drive is so invisible and seems to do so little work, why not hold to the earlier theory of drives?

Freud was ready with an answer in the final paragraph of part 4. The pleasure principle serves the id and the constancy principle dominates in a human organism. Having in mind Woodruff's work—which showed that the constant dividing of single-cell organisms, without stimulation from time to time (e.g., a change of nutritive fluid or a brief coalescence of cells), is likely not a process which promises eternality, but that coalescence, a primitive form of sexual interaction, works against cells' enfeeblement—Freud posited that "Eros . . . hold[s] up the falling level and introduce[s] fresh tensions" that ward off decay. In the human sexual act, the ejection of sexual substances is similar to the soma and germplasm. The similarity is alleged to be why "complete sexual satisfaction" is comparable to dying and why some animals die after copulation. That last sexual act eliminates Eros and gives the death drive free rein to bring the organism to an inorganic state—the greatest and final repetition (1923, *S.E.*, XIX: 46–47).

THE DEATH DRIVE AND CIVILIZED LIVING

Holowchak has argued in several publications[4] against the Grünbaumian thesis that Freud's metapsychology—"describing a psychical process in its dynamic, topographical and economic aspects" or forces, places, and quantities (1915, *S.E.*, XIV: 181)—always took a back seat to clinical matters—for example, that the metapsychological structure Freud so painstakingly crafted, rethought, crafted, etc., over the course of decades—was dispensable. Writes Grünbaum:

> It emerges clearly that when Freud unswervingly claimed natural science status for his theoretical constructions throughout his life, he did so first and foremost for his evolving clinical theory of personality and therapy, rather than for the metapsychology. For he had been chastened in his early reductionistic exuberance by the speedy demise of his "Project." And, once he had repudiated his ephemeral neurobiological model of the psyche after 1896, he perenni-

> ally saw himself entitled to proclaim the *scientificity* of his clinical theory *entirely on the strength of a secure and direct epistemic warrant from the observations he made of his patients and of himself.* In brief, during all but the first few years of his career, Freud's criterion of *scientificity* was *methodologically* and *not* ontologically reductive.[5]

Yet though Freud sometimes wrote of metapsychology as dispensable (e.g., 1914, *S.E.*, XIV: 77, and 1922, *S.E.*, XVIII; 253–54), he often also writes of its indispensability (e.g., 1925, *S.E.*, XX: 58–59, and 1939, *S.E.*, XXIII: 225). In short, "it gave his clinical data vindication through inclusion in a broad-ranging theoretical superstructure, not unlike that of Newtonian dynamics."[6] Moreover, it defies common sense to think that he would devote so much energy in mature years to works such as *Interpretation of Dreams*, "Repression," "The Unconscious," *Beyond the Pleasure Principle*, *The Ego and the Id*, and even *Civilization and Its Discontents* if his metapsychology was an expendable aspect of psychoanalysis. Further, any particular metapsychology may be dispensable without all metapsychologies being dispensable.

The "speculative" work *Beyond the Pleasure Principle* was a turning point, for better or worse, for Freud. Driven by complications concerning the compulsion to repeat which Freud could not accommodate to his original theory of ego drives and sexual drives, he provisionally posited a death drive. Three years later, he endorsed that drive and built it into his structural model.

Yet something else happens with *Beyond the Pleasure Principle*. Perhaps more than any other major work, it marks a shift, from emphasis on psychoanalysis as a curative technique in individual or clinical psychology to emphasis on psychoanalysis as prophylactic in group or social psychology, in Freud's thinking. We see that shift in emphasis in such significant works as *Group Psychology and the Analysis of the Ego* (1921), *The Future of an Illusion* (1927), and *Civilization and Its Discontents* (1930), although an interest in the clinical aspects of psychoanalysis remained until his death, but *Civilization and Its Discontents* is the focus of this section.

The introduction of the death drive to Freud's thinking was a theoretical breakthrough which enabled him to offer etiological explanations without, in his mind, incommoding other aspects of his metapsychological framework. The death drive enabled him, among other things, to extend the clinical observation that ambivalence is ubiquitous to an inductive posit of ambivalence as a fundamental aspect of a human organism.[7] The death drive permitted Freud to explicate punishment dreams and to have a better grasp of his old clinical enigmas: traumatic neurosis and narcissism.

Civilization and Its Discontents is today perhaps Freud's mostly widely read work. In it, he explained the rife discontent in civilized societies. What is the end of human living? That is a question for religion. What do humans take themselves to see as the end? That is supposedly happiness, which for

Freud can only be possible, in terms of drive theory, as "the (preferably sudden) satisfaction of needs which have been dammed up to a high degree, and it is from its nature only possible as an episodic phenomenon." Unhappiness, thus, is failure to release the dammed-up impulsive energy, and its chief courses are our own body through decay over time, the external world through unexpected "forces of destruction," and "our relations to other men" (1930, *S.E.*, XXI: 75–76). And so, the problem of happiness is at once "a problem of the economics of the individual's libido"[8] (1930, *S.E.*, XXI: 83).

Concerning our relations with others, healthy relationships might seem to be a consolation to buffer the unhappiness of bodily decay and of natural disasters, but healthy relationships are few. Thus, we buffer ourselves from unhappy relationships by voluntary isolation from others, intoxicants, efforts to control our drives (e.g., religious or moral precepts), illusions (e.g., indulgence in art or religion), and sublimated displacements (socially sanctioned work that allows for some small release of satisfaction of drives) (1930, *S.E.*, XXI: 76–83).

Yet our relations with others, experience shows, prove to be the greatest source of unhappiness. Why? Contrary to aging and natural disasters, our relations with others seem to be under our control. Still, "here, too, a piece of our own psychical constitution" prevents any sort of mastery of our relations. We reflect only to find that "what we call our civilization is largely responsible for our misery, and . . . we should be much happier if we gave it up and returned to primitive conditions," in which release of dammed-up impulse was more or less immediate. Civilization, by delaying or frustrating impulses, causes our unhappiness and our neuroses (1930, *S.E.*, XXI: 77–78).

What of the security civilization promises? Security comes at an agonizing price: delay or stoppage of gratification of impulses.

What of its technological advances? "Does it mean nothing that medicine has succeeded in enormously reducing infant mortality and the danger of infection for women in childbirth, and, indeed, in considerably lengthening the average life of a civilized man?" Freud waxed pessimistically. "Most of these satisfactions follow the model of the 'cheap enjoyment' extolled in the anecdote—the enjoyment obtained by putting a bare leg from under the bedclothes on a cold winter night and drawing it in again." First, without the railway "to conquer distances," our children would remain with us and we would not have to telephone them to hear their voice. Second, what of reduction of infant mortality? That imposes restrictions on the number of children we can birth, which "creates difficult conditions for our sexual life in marriage, and [has] probably worked against the beneficial effects of natural selection." Last, "what good to us is a long life if it is difficult and barren of joys, and if it is so full of misery that we can only welcome death as a deliverer?" (1930, *S.E.*, XXI: 88).

What then is civilization and how does it make us unhappy?

Civilization, claimed Freud, "describes the whole sum of the achievements and the regulations which distinguish our lives from those of our animal ancestors and which serves two purposes—namely to protect men against nature and to adjust their mutual relations" (1930, *S.E.*, XXI: 89). Man has done both in a remarkable degree. Whereas in the remote past, man ascribed remarkable powers, even omniety, to the gods, today "he has almost become a god himself." Yet, cautioned Freud, "not completely in some respects not at all, in others only half way." He continued: "Man has, as it were, become a kind of prosthetic God. When he puts on all his auxiliary organs he is truly magnificent; but those organs have not grown on to him and they still give him much trouble at times." He finds consolation that with further advances of civilization, he will become more like God and less of a prosthetic God. Still, "present-day man does not feel happy in his Godlike character" (1930, *S.E.*, XXI: 89–92).

Civilized men protect themselves against nature and regulate their relations by building canals, farming the soil, mining the land, exterminating dangerous animals and domesticating others, and improving intercommunications between men. Yet civilized men demand other, useless things: reverence of beauty, striving for cleanliness, and love of order which he saw in "the great astronomical regularities," which he replicated. "Order is a kind of compulsion to repeat which, when a regulation has been laid down once and for all, decides when, where and how a thing shall be done, so that in every similar circumstance one is spared hesitation and indecision" (1930, *S.E.*, XXI: 92–93).

What characterizes civilized man most, however, is his religious systems, philosophical speculations, and ideals—each a sublimation or partial frustration of libidinal aim. It is astonishing, added Freud, how much civilization is built on "a renunciation of instinct" (1930, *S.E.*, XXI: 94 and 97).

Thus far, Freud realized that he has said little regarding how society regulates human affairs. Consider liberty, so highly prized in Enlightenment days. It is, croaked Freud, "no gift of civilization." Men were freer prior to being civilized, but were then in no position to defend that freedom. As civilization advances, the number of restrictions on human freedom are greatened. Those restrictions recapitulate our passion for parsimony, order, and cleanliness—all characteristics of human anal character—in the "libidinal development of the individual" (1930, *S.E.*, XXI: 95–96).

Civilization, according to Freud, works by displacement. From being loved, people are taught to value loving. "They avoid the uncertainties and disappointments of genital love by turning away from its sexual aims and transforming the instinct into an impulse with an *inhibited* aim." The "stormy agitation of genital love" is supplanted by an "evenly suspended, steadfast, affectionate feeling." The aim is universal love. The result is a "severely impaired" sexual life (1930, *S.E.*, XXI: 102 and 105).

The civilizing creed is "Thou shalt love thy neighbor as thyself." The Golden Rule runs against the common sense view that to love all equally is to do one's friends a gross injustice. Moreover, that dissipates the affection I can have for any one person (1930, *S.E.*, XXI: 110).

Those telling objections notwithstanding, Freud has been leading up to a larger point. "The element of truth behind all this, which people are so ready to disavow, is that men are not gentle creatures who want to be loved, and who at the most can defend themselves if they are attacked; they are, on the contrary, creatures among whose instinctual endowments is to be reckoned a powerful share of aggression." Men are moved by a death drive (1930, *S.E.*, XXI: 111).

It is the death drive that "disturbs our relations with our neighbor and which forces civilization into such a high expenditure. In consequence of this primary mutual hostility of human beings, civilized society is perpetually threatened with disintegration." Common purpose and common work are of no avail, as "instinctual passions are stronger than reasonable interests." It is only through clever use of reaction-formations such as identifications and universal love that men's aggressive tendencies can be held in check. Humans, in effect, are willing to sacrifice "a portion of his possibilities of happiness for a portion of security" (1930, *S.E.*, XXI: 112 and 115).

In part 6, Freud turned to the drives. His early theory advanced ego drives and sex drives—the former, aiming at self-preservation; the latter, at species-preservation. "Neurosis was regarded as the outcome of a struggle between the interest of self-preservation and the demands of the libido, a struggle in which the ego had been victorious but at the price of severe sufferings and renunciations." Then came his "discovery" in narcissism that "the ego itself is cathected with libido." Then in 1920 there came the notion of Freud, drawing from the conservative nature of the drives and the compulsion to repeat, that there "must exist another, contrary instinct seeking to dissolve those units and to bring them back to their primaeval, inorganic state" (1930, *S.E.*, XXI: 117–18), if he was to make sense of his clinical observation.

Freud at first acknowledged that his revised views were only provisionally posited. Yet over time, his reservations evaporated. He claimed for these views that "they have gained such a hold upon me that I can no longer think in any other way." They are "more serviceable from a theoretical point of view" and "they provide that simplification, without either ignoring or doing violence to the facts, for which we strive in scientific work" (1930, *S.E.*, XXI: 119).

Two things follow from assuming a drive to unite and a drive to disunite. First, "civilization is a process in the service of Eros, whose purpose is to combine single human individuals, and after that families, then races, peoples and nations, into one great family." Second, "the inclination to aggression is an original, self-subsisting instinctual disposition in man" (1930, *S.E.*, XXI: 122). Freud drew the glum conclusion:

> The meaning of the evolution of civilization is no longer obscure to us. It must present the struggle between Eros and Death, between the instinct of life and the instinct of destruction, as it works itself out in the human species. This struggle is what all life essentially consists of, and the evolution of civilization may therefore be simply described as the struggle for life of the human species. And it is this battle of the giants that our nurse-maids try to appease with their lullaby about Heaven (1930, *S.E.*, XXI: 122).

The remainder of the book describe how civilization plays on man's sense of guilt, housed in each person's superego, to serve the process of higher-level binding of men with each other by renunciation of love objects, and to deflect outward destructive impulses. Neurosis has now become "substitutive satisfactions for unfulfilled sexual wishes." Moreover, the process of civilizing is "the repetition of the same formula" used to understand the development of an individual (1930, *S.E.*, XXI: 139). "If [civilizing] employs the same methods, may we not be justified in reaching the diagnosis that, under the influence of cultural urges, some civilizations, or some epochs of civilization—possibly the whole of mankind—have become 'neurotic'?" (1930, *S.E.*, XXI: 144).

Freud ended with a question concerning man's capacity to master the death drive so that he might eschew annihilation at his own hands (1930, *S.E.*, XXI: 145). He ends famously, "But who can foresee with what success and with what result?"

FREUD ON WAR

Freud directly addressed the topic of war on two separate occasions: the first, during World War I (1915); the second, several years prior to World War II (1932). To understand best his views in the later essay, which was written with the second theory of drives in mind, we first turn to the former, a significant contribution to the psychoanalytic view of human hatred, which was written with the early view of drives in mind.

In a 1915 paper titled "Timely Thoughts on War and Death," Freud wrote of our disillusionment during times of war. He began by distinguishing between "illusion" and "disillusion." Illusion is a wish-fulfillment fantasy that unlikely has a basis in reality. Disillusion is the destruction of an illusion. The distinction proves to be pivotal for his thesis (1915, *S.E.*, XIV: 275–76).

The onset of war challenges our sanity in two ways. First, a nation that demands of its citizenry utmost regard for morality exhibits utmost disregard for morality when warring with another nation. When not in the state of war, the state, claimed Freud, forbids its individuals the practice of wrongdoing. Yet that is not "because it desires to abolish it, but because it desires to monopolize it, like salt and tobacco." The state, when warring, treats its citizens like children through "an excess of secrecy and a censorship upon news and expressions of opinion." The state, negating treaties with other nations, exhibits a frightening "lust for power," under the guise of patriotism. Second and this point needs no amplification, individuals who have behaved civilly abandon civility during war and behave like angry beasts. Such sudden reversals, such sea changes as reaction-formations, are the result of ambivalence—the easy coexistence of contrary feelings like love and hate and the ready shift from one to the other—part of the fabric of the human constitution (1915, *S.E.*, XIV: 276 and 279–80).

Freud's explanation concerned human drives, which are neither good nor bad and are the same in all persons. Ego drives are deemed "bad" because they concern the self and work toward self-preservation, while sexual drives are deemed "good" because they concern our relations with others and work toward preservation of the species. Those drives undergo "a lengthy process of development" before they are active in adults. "By the admixture of *erotic* components the egoistic instincts are transformed into *social* ones," and humans "susceptibility to culture" is determined by success in that transformation (1915, *S.E.*, XIV: 281–83).

Civilized living is driven by erotic drives. The process of civilizing—here Freud anticipated his thesis in *Civilization and Its Discontents*—"demands good conduct" and does not concern itself with expression of impulses. "Society has allowed itself to be misled into tightening the moral standard to the greatest possible degree, and it has thus forced its members into a yet greater estrangement from their instinctual disposition." In effect, society uses humans' impulses against its citizens in an effort to engender socially appropriate, "moral" behavior. It plays on humans' need for love and their feelings of worthlessness to prompt conformity to social rules. It demands renunciation of human impulses—e.g., "Thou shall not kill" and "Thou shall not commit adultery" (impulses that cry out for expression)—in exchange for conformity, and ultimately, security. The cost is prodigious. The result is often "the reactive phenomena of neurotic disorders" (1915, *S.E.*, XIV: 283–84).

War is an opportunity for drives to be given free rein. "Our mortification and our painful disillusionment" concerning our uncivilized behavior during times of war are unfounded. "They were based on an illusion to which we had given way. In reality our fellow-citizens have not sunk so low as we feared, because they had never risen so high as we believed" (1915, *S.E.*, XIV: 285).

Freud was never all that comfortable with this explanation. What was the reason? It is difficult to see how all the extraordinary atrocities of war could merely be the result of the frustration of sexual impulses. With his new theory of drives, adopted formally in 1923, Freud would be readied to provide a simpler answer.

In 1931, the International Institute of Intellectual Cooperation instructed by the Permanent Committee for Literature and the Arts (of the League of Nations) arranged for the exchange of letters between prominent scholars and scientists. Einstein was approached and he suggested Freud as his correspondent on the topic of war.

Einstein wrote to Freud on July 30, 1932.

Freud replied sometime in September, 1932. He began by admission that he agreed with most of what Einstein had written—"violence overcome by the transference of power to a larger unity, which is held together by emotional ties between members"—and could only "amplify" Einstein's sentiments. (1932, *S.E.*, XXII: 203 and 205).

Freud considered war as a vehicle for perpetual peace.

> Paradoxical as it may sound, it must be admitted that war might be a far from inappropriate means of establishing the eagerly desired rein of 'everlasting' peace, since it is in a position to create the large units within which a powerful central government makes further wars impossible. Nevertheless it fails in this purpose, for the results of conquest are as a rule short-lived: the newly created units fall apart once again, usually owing to a lack of cohesion between the portions that have been united by violence. (1932, *S.E.*, XXII: 206)

Yet that process only leads both to larger "units" in opposition to each other and to wars at a larger scale. "Wars will only be prevented with certainly if mankind unites in setting up a central authority to which the right of giving judgment upon all conflicts of interest shall be handed over" (1932, *S.E.*, XXII: 207).

Such things noted, Freud turned to human beings' zeal for war. Here he was armed with his new theory of drives. "According to our hypothesis human instincts are of only two kinds: those which seek to preserve and unite—which we call 'erotic' . . . or 'sexual,' with a deliberate extension of the popular conception of 'sexuality'—and those which seek to destroy and kill and which we group together as the aggressive or destructive instinct." This fundamental human ambivalence of love and hate Freud likened to the attraction and repulsion in physics (1932, *S.E.*, XXII: 209).

Eros and the death drives do not function independently of each other. "An instinct of the one sort can scarcely ever operate in isolation; it is always accompanied—or, as we say, alloyed—with a certain quota from the other side, which modifies its aim or is, in some cases, what enables it to achieve that aim." Love requires a quota of aggression to achieve its aim. So too does self-preservation (1932, *S.E.*, XXII: 209–10).

The interplay of drives is complex. For every human action, "there must be as a rule a combination of such compounded motives. . . . When human beings are incited to war they may have a whole number of motives for assenting—some noble and some base, some which are openly declared and others which are never mentioned." He added, "A lust for aggression and destruction is certainly among them." Freud explained how wartime atrocities (e.g., the Inquisition) are rationalized by "idealistic motives" (1932, *S.E.*, XXII: 210).

Consequently, it is impossible to eradicate destructive impulses. "There is no question of getting rid entirely of human aggressive impulses; it is enough to try to divert them to such an extent that they need not find expression in war." Freud considered two deflective strategies—"two *indirect* methods of combating war." First, humans can do what they can to bring Eros into play, as an antagonist, against the death drive. This suggestion is to cultivate universal love of others and to pursue identification through shared feelings and interests. That is a solution he outright rejected in *Civilization and Its Discontents* as not only impracticable, but also unjust. Second, human beings can do what they can to take the death drive out of play, insofar as that is possible through deflection strategies. "The ideal condition of things would of course be a community of men who had subordinated their instinctual life to the dictatorship of reason. . . . But that in all probability is a Utopian expectation" (1932, *S.E.*, XXII: 212–13).

Freud concluded, "An unpleasant picture comes to one's mind of mills that grind so slowly that people may starve before they get their flour." He ended by mentioning a benefit of civilization. "One thing we can say: whatever fosters the growth of civilization works at the same time against war" (1932, *S.E.*, XXII: 213–15). The sentiment runs against the thesis of *Civilization and Its Discontents*, which promises greater unhappiness with the advances of civilization, but perhaps a peaceful, civilized unhappiness is better than the inevitable alternative of nations at war.

NOTES

1. For more, see M. Andrew Holowchak, *Freud: From Individual Psychology to Group Psychology* (Lanham, MD: Jason Aronson, 2012), 19 ff.
2. This is a view with which Freud earlier tinkered over ten years. "I cannot bring myself to assume the existence of a special aggressive instinct alongside of the familiar instincts of self-preservation and of sex, and on an equal footing with them" (1909, *S.E.*, X: 140),
3. These seem to be strange claims, as psychoanalysis is committed to there being no such thing as erotic indifference. Freud recognizes that, and adds that the ego is peculiar apropos of the choice of object and the manner of discharge (1923, *S.E.*, XIX: 45).
4. See especially, *Freud and Utopia: From Cosmological Narcissism to the Soft Dictatorship of Reason* (Lanham, MD: Lexington Books, 2012), 23–25, and *Freud: From Individual to Group Psychology* (Lanham, MD: Jason Aronson, 2012), 105–12.
5. Adolph Grünbaum, *Foundations of Psychoanalysis*, 5–6.
6. M. Andrew Holowchak, *Freud*, 111.
7. In *Three Essays on a Theory of Sexuality*, sadism was merely a component impulse of the sexual drive (1905, *S.E.*, VII: 158).

8. He curiously fails to mention aggression in his discussion of economics.

III

Critical Analysis

Chapter Six

Freud's Compulsion to Justify the Death Drive

As we have seen, the provisional status of the death drive in *Beyond the Pleasure Principle* is given Freud's full-fledged patronage three years later in *The Ego and the Id*, where Freud has two sustained discussions of it, minus any reference to his conjecture of a "daemonic" compulsion to repeat. The unqualified patronage is mysterious, given numerous problems with both concepts.

We begin this chapter with some discussion of that omission in *The Ego and the Id*, and then turn to a critical analysis of Freud's view of the death drive in a 1932 paper, "Anxiety and Instinctual Life." The remainder of the chapter is a critical discussion of Freud's belief in the theoretical indispensability of the death drive, of Eros and the death drive as telic principles, and of the compulsion to repeat in service of the death drive.

A CURIOUS OMISSION

We begin with a brief discussion of what is not so much a problem, but a curious omission—the lack of any reference to the compulsion to repeat in *The Ego and the Id*. In *Beyond the Pleasure Principle*, the compulsion to repeat is central among the considerations that persuaded Freud of the existence of the death drive. Whatever merit the postulation of a death drive has in 1920 it has that merit mostly because of its link to the compulsion to repeat in relation to the pleasure principle. Sometimes, observed Freud, a compulsion to repeat is indicative of behavior inconsistent with the primacy of the pleasure principle. Thus such daemonic compulsions to repeat took center stage and pointed ineluctably to a destructive drive. Why then does Freud not mention the compulsion to repeat in 1923, when he went all in for the death drive?

One might argue that Freud's aims while writing *The Ego and the Id* are different. In 1923, he was focusing on the nature of the psychical agencies of his emerging structural model, and how to accommodate the structural model to his emerging theory of dual drives, and how both are related to psychopathological phenomena such as the alleged, now rejected, link between persecutory paranoia and homosexuality, not a justification of the death drive per se. In 1920, he was struggling to have a better grasp of clinical phenomena, which struck him as incompatible with his standing account of the pleasure principle. As mentioned, certain types of compulsive repetitions seemed, to Freud, incompatible with his standing account of the pleasure principle, and seemed to require an inference to a better explanation that involved explicit recognition of a death drive. These clinical worries notwithstanding, it is still odd that there is no mention of the compulsion to repeat in 1923.

Freud gave many examples of behaviors illustrative of the compulsion to repeat, even if not so tagged, in *Beyond the Pleasure Principle*—children's play, resistance in therapy, casual observations of human behavior, "fated" repetitions, and dreams of patients with traumatic neuroses—including some claimed to necessitate the hypothesis of the death drive. What distinguishes examples which are justificatory of the death drive—resistance in therapy, casual observations, "fated" repetition, and dreams of patients with traumatic neurosis—from examples which are not, such as children's play?

Freud's answer was that compulsively repetitive behaviors characteristic of the death drive are a daemonic dimension of human behavior that is inconsistent with the pleasure principle. Therefore an inference to a plausible and sound explanation requires some other driving force than the pleasure principle exists. If so, then nothing further needs to be said on behalf of the death drive: Daemonic instances of the compulsion to repeat are better understand if an inference to a best explanation is made. Like all inferences to the best explanation, the inference is defeasible. So, the inference to the existence of a death drive in cases where the pleasure principle fails to save the clinical phenomena saves the phenomena rather than seeks to explain them away. We shall return to this unresolved issue at chapter's end.

DEATH DRIVE REDUX, 1932

Freud returned to the death drive yet again in a 1932 paper, "Anxiety and Instinctual Life," from his *New Introductory Lectures on Psychoanalysis*. There he promised readers that he had new insights concerning "our conception [*Auffassung*] of anxiety and the basic instincts of mental life." His choice of the vague *Auffassung*, where a precise term might be apposite, was intentional. "It is truly a matter of conceptions—that is to say, of introducing the right abstract ideas, whose application to the raw material of observation will produce order and clarity" (1932, *S.E.*, XXII: 81). Here, however, it is theory molding facts, not raw facts suggesting a theory.

Freud wrote of fresh insights on anxiety. "Anxiety . . . is the reproduction of an old event which brought a threat of danger [and] anxiety serves the purposes of self-preservation and is a signal of a new danger." He distinguished between realistic and neurotic anxiety—the former being graspable as a reaction to an anticipated danger (viz., a venomous insect entering a room); the latter being "completely enigmatic," but by implication something internal to the anxious person (viz., a proscribed unconscious wish or impulse) Vis-à-vis the former, "the repetition of the old trauma" manifests itself as a signal and the organism can adapt by fight or flight, or "the old situation can retain the upper hand and the anxiety generated becomes paralytic. Vis-à-vis the latter, first, there can be a freely floating general apprehensiveness that attaches itself to "any possibility that may freshly arise"; second, apprehensiveness can be firmly attached to distinct ideas as in the phobias wherein the fear of external danger might be real but is "exaggerated out of all proportion"; and last, there is anxiety in neuroses which may accompany symptoms or emerge independently without external provocation (1932, *S.E.*, XXII: 81–82 and 84).

What is the explanation of neurotic anxiety? Consistent with prior etiological explanations, one might guess the most common cause is frustration of sexual impulses. Yet there is a second explanation, not unrelated to the first: repression. Here there is a separation of the idea, requiring repression, and the quota of energy, linked with it. The idea is relegated to the unconscious and the energy, whether of a libidinal or destructive sort, "is regularly transformed into anxiety." In reality, those mechanisms coincide (1932, *S.E.*, XXII: 82–83).

Freud illustrated through phobias and obsessional neurosis. In agoraphobia, for instance, a patient may feel anxiety by walking on the street, and "this would be repeated every time he went into the street again." He is spared anxiety by refraining from going into the street. The converse occurs in obsessions, where a patient is spared anxiety by repetition of an obsessional, ritualistic behavior. Here prevention of a ritual results in anxiety (1932, *S.E.*, XXII: 83–84).

Yet something is still missing from the libidinal picture. Whereas Freud formerly assumed that anxiety is caused by repression, whether realistic or neurotic, he now maintains that anxiety is the indirect cause of sustained repression, as it elicits defenses to lower the anxiety by "fending off" the emergence into consciousness of the impulse or wish setting off the alarm that is signal anxiety (fear). Furthermore, the traumatizing event is in most cases real—the actual fantasy of a threat of castration—and that "has given our conviction a last degree of certainty." He added, "Neurotic anxiety has changed in our hands into realistic anxiety." Again, in all cases of the generation of anxiety, the ego, which is weak in comparison with the id, "is the sole seat of anxiety" (1932, *S.E.*, XXII: 85–87, 89, and 93), and that is because it is, on reflection, the sole plausible locus for anxiety as neither the id nor superego is a possible locus.

There is a final step. "What is feared, what is the object of the anxiety, is invariably the emergence of a traumatic moment, which cannot be dealt with by the normal rules of the pleasure principle." He added: "We shall no longer maintain that it is the libido itself that is turned into anxiety in such cases. . . . I can see no objection to there being a twofold origin of anxiety—one as a direct consequence of the traumatic moment and the other as a signal threatening a repetition of such a moment" (1932, *S.E.*, XXII: 94–95). Freud has thus set the stage for a discussion of the death drive.

"The theory of instincts," claimed Freud, "is so to say our mythology." People, it is commonly observed, flippantly and in an ad hoc manner, use impulses to solve any problem and explain any otherwise inexplicable behavior. Acknowledging their ad hoc use, Freud conceded, "in our work we cannot for a moment disregard them" (1932, *S.E.*, XXII: 95).

Freud began a lengthy "trite repetition" to function as a starting point for psychoanalytic advances in the theory of drives—a repetition needed as a springboard for a "report on the advances in our knowledge [of drives]" (1932, *S.E.*, XXII: 99–102).

In the original theory of drives, the ego drives and sex drives were thought to work independently of each other. Then Freud's work with narcissistic patients forced him to notice a new theoretical challenge. The problem of narcissism, where sexual libido was converted to ego libido, and other problems in which ego libido was converted to sexual libido, seemed to him to make his current theory of drives uneasy to accommodate to the clinical facts. That all-too-easy conversion of sexual to ego libido suggested the two drives "could not be different in their nature and it could have no sense to distinguish the energy of the one from the energy of the other." The only alternative was to replace "libido" with some other term or have it connote "psychical energy in general" (1932, *S.E.*, XXII: 102–3).

Things soon changed, and a new dualism emerged. The ego drives and sex drives—seen as manifestations of the same energy, hence being the same drive—were subsumed under Eros, while set in opposition to Eros were the aggressive drives, aiming at dissolution (1932, *S.E.*, XXII: 103).

This new view of drives, noted Freud, met with rapid opposition—a sign of a strong affective resistance, and for a good reason. Why, asked Freud rhetorically, has psychoanalysis taken so long to recognize that death drive, if it is so fundamental? That is on account of the naïve human belief that humans "are naturally good or at least good-natured." Yet that view flies in the face of history. Moreover, consider the phenomena of sadism and masochism. "Both phenomena, sadism and masochism alike, but masochism quite especially, present a truly puzzling problem to the libido theory; and it is only proper if what was a stumbling-block for the one theory should become the corner-stone of the theory replacing it" (1932, *S.E.*, XXII: 103–4).

Masochism, following Freud's biological evidence in *Beyond the Pleasure Principle*, must pre-date sadism, which is merely the primitive destructive impulse, deflected outward and becoming aggressiveness. Yet that scenario, because of the erotic (binding) principles of civilized living, might not be often actualized, and if so, that might prove debilitating for humans (1932, *S.E.*, XXII: 105–6).

Freud was admitting to evidence for the death drive being slender. He appealed to the conservative nature of all drives. "We may suppose that from the moment at which a state of things that has once been attained is upset, an instinct arises to create it afresh and brings about phenomena which we can describe as a 'compulsion to repeat.'" Freud listed such manifestations in the organic world, and he expanded on the list of behaviors manifesting the compulsion to repeat that he gave in 1920. He noted that embryology, the capacity to regenerate lost organs, the ability to recover from illness, the spawning of fishes, the migratory flights of birds, and perhaps even everything called "instinct" (here, *Instinkt*) in animals are manifestations of the "conservative nature of the instincts" (here, *Triebe*).

There are problems.

First, there is Freud's conflation of terms, which is not captured by Strachey, who translated both *Instinkt* and *Trieb* in the passage as "instinct." Freud has chosen *Trieb* and not *Instinkt* for his metapsychological uses, because the latter is strictly a biological concept, but the former is a psychobiological concept, serviceable for metapsychology—"a concept on the frontier between the mental and the somatic" (1915, *S.E.*, XIV: 121–22). All the illustrations he gave in "Anxiety and Instinctual Life" are *Instinkten*, not *Triebe.* Why then does Freud here use the terms interchangeably or unthinkingly? Moreover, given Freud's preference for *Trieb* in the psychobiological realm, what assurance can we have that what is true of *Instinkten* in the organic world is likewise true of *Triebe* in the psycho-biological world of humans? Recall here Freud's guardedness in 1920 about drawing inferences so much from the realm of biology to suit metapsychological needs (1920, *S.E.*, XVIII: 60). Freud is committed to the claim that what is true of certain instincts—that they are compulsions to repeat—is also true of drives.

Worse still, none of these examples solve psychological riddles that are at the center of Freud's work. If the earlier survey of Freud's use of "repetition" shows anything, it is that a core meaning involves a disguised, in some sense psychically satisfying, re-presentation in adulthood of childhood wishes and impulses, usually centering on sexuality, that are now banned from adult consciousness. With the arrival of the compulsion to repeat, there arises the idea that some repetitions, daemonic and compulsive ones, are at odds with the pleasure principle. A derivative of this idea remains to this day in the DSM requirement that compulsions are *not* compulsions if the behavior involved with them is pleasurable. By contrast, impulsive behaviors, for example drinking and gambling, are pleasurable and can become addictions.

In the mental field of humans, continued Freud, repressed, unpleasant experiences find expression in patients' dreams in the transference relationship. "We have explained this by supposing that in these cases a compulsion to repeat is overcoming even the pleasure principle." Moreover, "there are people in whose lives the same reactions are perpetually being repeated uncorrected, to their own detriment, or others who seem to be pursued by a relentless fate," though the fate is of their doing. Those are instances of "a 'daemonic' character to the compulsion to repeat" (1932, *S.E.*, XXII: 106–7).

In the human realm, elements in dreams, reactions in analysis, common repetitive behaviors outside of analysis, and even "fated" repetitions are manifestations of the compulsion to repeat and human self-destructiveness (1932, *S.E.*, XXII: 106–7). Conspicuously absent is children's play, unquestionably given as an instance of the compulsion to repeat twelve years earlier (1920, *S.E.*, XVIII: 23). Freud never showed why these observed repetitions, especially those instances of nonhuman repetitions, essentially involve a violation of the pleasure principle. Perhaps, he thinks it is plain. For example, a doctor can elicit an instinctive reflex, for example a patellar reflex occurs independently of any pleasure or displeasure. Likewise, sheep in a herd instinctively will follow the Judas sheep, even if it is to their doom. Nevertheless, it is anything but plain that the cited repetitions are incompatible with the pleasure principle, though one possibility is that paradigmatic child's play is not regressive while the other examples are.[1] In addition and consistent with the introduction of the compulsion repeat is the idea that play does not require a clinical "working through."[2] It is not an example from psychoanalytic psychopathology. Much child's play is far from innocent, as anybody who has seen decapitated dolls knows.

It is the conservative nature of the drives—they wish to restore an earlier state of affairs—which forced upon Freud the death drive. "If it is true that—at some immeasurably remote time and in a manner we cannot conceive—life once proceeded out of inorganic matter, then, according to our presumption, an instinct must have arisen which sought to do away with life once more and to reestablish the inorganic state." And so, there must be an impulse to restore what is organic to what is inorganic, and that drive "cannot fail to be present in every vital process." Thus, there is Eros, a force which combines living things into increasingly greater units, and there are the death drives, "which oppose this effort and lead what is living back into an inorganic state" (1932, *S.E.*, XXII: 107). Concerning how the two drives, present in the impulse toward any human action, are soldered to bring about human activity Freud has little to say.

Here Freud's argument, listed above and fleshed out below, is strained.

1. At some immeasurably remote time, organisms came from inorganic matter.
2. Human drives are conservative—that is, they wish to repeat or restore an early state of affairs.
3. So, there must be a drive to return to or restore what is inorganic from what is organic.

It is essentially the same argument given in *Beyond the Pleasure Principle* and equally paralogistic. Premise 1 is quite reasonable. Few biologists today, except mavericks, would deny it. Yet premise 2 is not. Let us take Eros, which "repeats" by continually striving to unite things into greater organic units. These repetitions are, strictly speaking, not repetitions of redundancy, but vector repetitions that move in the direction of increased unification. Moreover, granting premise 2, the conclusion does not follow unless there are several other premises assumed.

1. At some immeasurably remote time, organisms came from inorganic matter.
2. That process was repeated innumerable times.
3. When any natural process is repeated innumerable times that process is a manifestation of a natural drive—a natural conservative tendency of things.
4. So, such a process of organic repetition can only be the result of a drive.
5. All individual organisms perish or decay over time.
6. That process too is a repetition.
7. So, that process too is a manifestation of a drive.
8. So, there must be a drive to return to or restore what is inorganic from what is organic.

Does Freud have something like this argument in mind, though he expresses himself unhelpfully economically? Here we may be charitable, or perhaps uncharitable, and say, "Yes," given what we have seen in *Beyond the Pleasure Principle*, where some of the argument is analogical, and based on biologists observing infusoria.[3]

Still there is something strained in the second part of the argument, which seeks to establish the death drive. We can acknowledge an erotic drive and the truth of premise 5 without needing to posit a death drive. The decay or perishing of individual organisms along the way might merely be an indication of an imperfect process or a process ever perfecting itself by degrees.

IS THE DEATH DRIVE INDISPENSABLE?

As we have seen in *Beyond the Pleasure Principle* and in works thereafter, Freud kept insisting on the theoretical indispensability of the death drive. He claimed not to be able to proceed without it. The observations themselves cannot otherwise be glued together. In 1920, he said, "It is impossible to pursue an idea of this kind except by repeatedly combining factual material with what is purely speculative and thus diverging widely from empirical observation." Yet he claimed merely to be "an *advocatus diaboli*, who is not on that account himself sold to the devil" (1920, *S.E.* XVIII: 59). In later works, he sold himself to the devil. In *The Ego and the Id*, he said, "Without assuming the existence of a displaceable energy of this kind we can make no headway" (1923, *S.E.*, XIX: 44). He also claimed that the fusion of the two in each living particle is "an assumption indispensable to our conception" (1923, *S.E.*, XIX: 41). Thus, the gain of the metapsychological posit of a death drive has a theoretical yield: It ties up otherwise loose ends.

Is that correct?

The general view in the secondary literature is that the death drive creates more problems than it solves. Consider this litany of objections put forth by Peter Kramer:

> How can a death drive, present from birth, aid an animal's survival? Neither is it intuitive that a *Todestrieb* explains shell shock. If we are instinctively drawn to death, why is war traumatic? But the oddest feature of the unpleasure principle is its relationship to the rest of Freud's carefully nurtured theory. If self-destructiveness is inborn, then we have no need of an Oedipus complex to explain neurosis and no need for ambivalence toward the beloved to explain depression.[4]

What Kramer hints at is that Freud's death drive makes many other features of his theory de trop. It is a view we share and shall cash out as we address Freud's several arguments for the indispensability of the death drive.

If we follow his line of thinking on narcissism, we find that the convertible energy that can be used sexually or for the purposes of the ego is for Freud evidence not of two kinds of energy, each of which can be converted into the other, but of an undifferentiated kind of energy which can be used for narcissistic or sexual purposes. Where there is one sort of energy—whether it is called libido is irrelevant—there is one sort of drive.

Recall, in *Beyond the Pleasure Principle*, that that scenario itself was unwelcome for Freud. First, psychoanalysts would be prey to the objection that psychotherapy is pansexualist. Freud could eschew that objection by positing a drive in opposition to Eros. Second, Freud said that psychoanalysis has always been nakedly dualistic. "Our views have from the very first been *dualistic*, and to-day they are even more definitely dualistic than before" (1920, *S.E.*, XVIII: 52–53). The use of the comparative "more" may be taken to be indicative of a greater degree of conviction on Freud's part on the existence of two drives, now starkly antagonistic or perhaps as a clue that Freud thought his new dualism had greater range than his old dualism.

If the two replies are to be taken as arguments for a death drive—and we profess that that is the best way to take them—they are horrific arguments. To the first objection, we say, so what if critics object that psychoanalysis is pansexualist, so long as we understand "sexuality" in a broad sense to cover both ego- and sex-impulses? Freud never backed away from sexual criticisms before. For instance, it was his strong belief that all cases of hysteria, in his work with Breuer, had a sexual etiology. So, why should pansexualism be so crushing? To the second objection, we say that Freud is forcing theoretical preferences to facts onto which they do not so neatly fit. It might be that he has a predilection for dualism come what may, but facts are stubborn things, and it must be factual considerations, not theoretical prejudices, which drive any modifications of his metapsychological frame. A preference for two drives instead of one is not an argument for the death drive.[5]

Then there is the problem of hate, which formerly was explained by there being a sadistic component in the sexual drive. That maneuver seemed ad hoc, said Freud, if we concede that humans seem to hate about as much as they love. Recall in *The Ego and the Id* that Freud observed in analysis that the shift from love to hate and hate to love occurred with astonishing rapidity and regularity. With the new theory of drives, Freud could appeal etiologically to a primary, impulsive ambivalence.

Yet the rapid and ready shift from love to hate and hate to love can be explicated, according to the first theory of drives, by frustration of erotic aims, in the former instance, and by anticipation of success of frustrated erotic aims, in the second. And so, we do not need primary ambivalence.

Furthermore, let us follow up on another of Kramer's objections: The death drive is effete in clinical practice. "Sexual repression can be lifted, freeing the patient to enjoy genital fulfillment. But satisfying the death drive is incompatible with successful treatment."[6]

Following the dual aims of Eros as a drive to preserve individuals and the species, the death drive is an impulse directed to destruction of individuals, and, directed outward, of the species. How is an analyst to work economically with the demands of the death drive, which must be as trying as those of Eros, though they are much harder to recognize? Freud said nothing about that. He tends to eschew all nontheoretical discussion of the death drive. It comes into discussion only in metapsychological, not clinical, discussions.

For all intents and purposes, psychoanalytic therapy is exclusively (or mostly so) concerned with the mind in conflict.

Finally, there is the problem of regulating the demands of the death drive in societies. That proves to be a large problem—one with no simple solution. Recall in "Why War?" the proposed solutions were to cultivate Eros through universal love of men—a solution he deemed both impracticable and unjust in 1930—and to deflect destructive impulses in a socially acceptable or at least condonable manner. Yet the issue of economics—*viz.*, the relative quotas of the erotic and death drives in the species—was at the rear of Freud's mind, and he left us with the picture of a mill grinding so slowly that people starved before they got any food.

THE TELIC NODUS

Freud was always insistent that there were a large number of drives in all living organisms. The question for him was whether those drives could be traceable to substratal drives, and if so, how many were there. In "The Theory of the Instincts" from his posthumously published *Outline of Psycho-Analysis*, he stated, "After long hesitancies and vacillations we have decided to assume the existence of only two basic instincts, *Eros* and *the destructive instinct*." This assumption, coming roughly twenty years after *Beyond the Pleasure Principle*, is neither a strong commitment to dualism nor an unrevokable commitment to the destructive or death drive.

Freud described the substratal drives. Concerning Eros, he wrote, "The aim of the first of these basic instincts is to establish ever greater unities and to preserve them thus—in short, to bind together." Concerning the destructive drive, he wrote, "the aim of the second is, on the contrary, to undo connections and so to destroy things. . . . We may suppose that its final aim is to lead what is living into an inorganic state" (1940, *S.E.*, XXIII: 148).

Yet Eros is not merely a binding and preserving drive, but a drive that aims at increasing complexity while binding and preserving. An aim implies a telos for Eros. That is consistent with a trend today by physicists, biologists, and other scientists who claim that natural selection works over time to select for complexity of organic systems. Daniel Wolpert maintains that complexity is not only consistent with the second law of thermodynamics, which decreases complexity in closed systems, but also that it is what drives complexity in open subsystems.[7] Physicist Paul Davies writes, "If we take as a measure of complexity change, not successive instantaneous sums over all extant species, but the directionality of branching, then there is clearly, for unexceptional reasons, a growth of complexity with time."[8] John Maynard Smith and Eörs Sathmáry, in their book *The Major Transitions of Evolution*, argue that living organisms' "complexity has increased in the course of evolution" and that "the increase has depended on a small number of major transitions."[9] Börgje Ekstig, noting that species once emerged tend to "persist almost unchanged" till extinction, asserts that that persistency is consistent with natural selection working toward higher levels of biological complexity.[10] Finally, psychologist Martin Seligman argues that the increasing complexity toward which natural selection works—"this increasing complexity [is] identical with greater power and greater knowledge . . . [and as] greater goodness, since goodness is about a ubiquitous group of virtues that all successful cultures have evolved"[11]—is evidence that "in human history, we are going from knowledge to omniscience, from potence to omnipotence, and from ethics and religion to righteousness." Humans, it appears, are part of a process of becoming God—emergent theism—and we can choose to "be a small part of furthering this process."[12]

Freud disavowed any such talk of a telos to living systems. Such speculations, metempirical, were beyond the ken of an above board scientist. "The efforts of Eros to combine organic substances into ever larger unities," wrote Freud in a 1923 addition to *Beyond the Pleasure Principle*, "probably provide a substitute for this 'instinct towards perfection' whose existence we cannot admit." That "perfecting" is explicable by the efforts of Eros taken in conjunction with the results of repression" (1920, *S.E.*, XVIII: 45–46). Yet we can only say, "Why?" Much of what he said about the death drive is motivated by metapsychological considerations, and there is more that is philosophical than empirical in such considerations.

Freud also wrote teleologically concerning the death drive. The aim of the pleasure principle "is to free the mental apparatus entirely from excitation or to keep it as low as possible," which is also close to a definition of his old Principle of Constancy. The death drive ultimately works in conjunction with the pleasure principle, for its function is "the most universal endeavor of all living substance—namely to return to the quiescence of the inorganic world." He illustrated with the sexual act, which is "a momentary extinction of a highly intensified excitation." Thus the moment of death is similarly a discharge—"its final elimination in the pleasure of discharge" (1920, *S.E.*, XVIII: 62).

Cordelia Schmidt-Hellerau agrees. The new definition is finalistic or telic—"an *intelligent* magnitude that *knows* what it wants and *remembers* what it has seen." Thus drive is now structural—characteristic of the system as a whole—not a particular variable of it. Therefore one can no longer speak of *Eros* and the death drive as equal and antagonistic. On this reading, the death drive is *tout court* primary; drive dualism loses its meaning, or is at least far removed from Freud's elaboration of it through the 1920s and 1930s.[13] The death drive, it seems, holds the only trump card in the deck.

Schimdt-Hellerau is perhaps a bit hasty. Eros has its say, if only through those intense moments of "extinction of a highly intensified excitation." In that manner, an organism lives to the next generation in the only possible manner.

Edward Bibring also would have agreed. "So long as the concept of aim was used merely as a criterion for classification," it was consistent with drive as a quantitative concept. With aim introduced, the notion of drive as quantitative became problematic. "To do so involved turning the instincts into mental *qualities* and restricting their *quantitative* aspect to each separate group of them."[14]

Freud was aware of such criticisms. In "The Economic Problem of Masochism," Freud considered the constancy principle in light of the pleasure principle: "Every unpleasure ought thus to coincide with a heightening, and every pleasure with a lowering, of mental tension due to stimulus" (1924, *S.E.*, XIX: 159–60).

Then there is the interplay between Eros and the mostly unobtrusive death drive. "In biological functions the two basic instincts operate against each other or combine with each other." He discussed eating and sex as examples. In eating, the object eaten is destroyed through consummation, yet in consummation, there is incorporation of the object eaten. The sexual act, in contrast, "is an act of aggression with the purpose of the most intimate union" (1940, *S.E.*, XXIII: 149).

The examples are again tendentious, fit to accommodate his second theory of drives. Do we eat for the purpose of destruction—to satisfy, in part, a destructive impulse? Cannot eating be satisfactorily explained by ego drives and sex drives—that by eating, we obey the drive toward self-preservation, and that destruction of, say, a pig in the process is merely and exclusively a means to an end, not in part an end in itself—that is, satisfaction of an urge to destroy? Moreover, is sex always and essentially aggressive? Do all instances, say, of penetration in the act of sex satisfy an urge to destroy as well as an urge to unite?[15] Many will say love making need not be an act of aggression, but it can be a tender moment shared.[16]

THE COMPULSION TO REPEAT AND THE DEATH DRIVE

Edward Bibring thought the compulsion to repeat was a needed psychoanalytic concept—"a general regulative principle [which] serves to bind energies" and the "*sine qua non* of all the other regulative trends."[17]

Yet there are problems of the compulsion to repeat and of how it relates to the death drive.

First, if we take "compulsion" (*Zwang*) in one way it is lexically defined—as a strong and in general irresistible impulse to perform an act, usually without the sanction of will—then in what way are instincts and drives *compulsive* repetitions? What is compulsive in an animal regenerating a lost limb? Animals with that capacity just do it without knowing that it is being done or feeling any irresistible impulse in the process. What is likewise compulsive about birds migrating? "Compulsion," thus defined, implies a struggle of some sort or a battle lost. Moreover, in the realm of human behavior, Freud noted that children at play tirelessly repeat the same game or some form of play, as they find pleasure in mastery through repetition. There is nothing here beyond the pleasure principle, and it is hard to see how repetitions in the service of the pleasure principle can be compulsive.[18]

The problem is acute because Freud never offers a precise definition of *Wiederholungszwang*, serviceable for his new science. He failed to distinguish between repetitive behavior and compulsive repetitive behavior. As Dobson and Katchan write, "The constant repetition of a behavior—irrespective of whether it is stimulated by the experiencing representative of a traumatic event—does not imply the existence of a 'compulsion to repeat,' as distinguished from the 'compulsion which leads to the behavior itself.'"[19] In short, what gives certain *Wiederholungen* their *Zwang*?

Again, the manner in which the compulsion to repeat is a signifier of the death drive is suspicious. Freud noted, in the case of the dreams of persons suffering with traumatic neuroses, that the repetitions place them back into the situation that caused their neurosis. He wrote: "We may assume, rather, that dreams are here helping to carry out another task, which must be accomplished before the dominance of the pleasure principle can even begin. Their dreams are endeavouring to master the stimulus retrospectively, by developing the anxiety whose omission was the cause of the traumatic neurosis." Such dreams are retrospective attempts to master the traumatic situation by bringing forth the anxiety that is claimed to accompany traumatic events. So, they aim to bring persons to a state where they can once again experience pleasure. "They thus afford us a view of a function of the mental apparatus which, though it does not contradict the pleasure principle, is nevertheless independent of it and seems to be more primitive than the purpose of gaining pleasure and avoiding pain" (1920, *S.E.*, XVIII: 31–32).[20]

Two things here are worth noting. First, Freud stated baldly that some repetitive, traumatic dreams are not inconsistent with the pleasure principle. If they are not inconsistent, how is it that they offer evidence of something beyond the pleasure principle? Second, some repetitive behaviors, which are an attempt to master a traumatic situation, can be viewed as defensive struggles to master traumatic situations. If mastery serves the function of allowing an organism to experience future pleasure without obstacles, then how do such struggles offer straightforward evidence of a death drive? Of course the answer would be easy if one knew, as we do not, the quantity of pleasure from mastery versus the pain endured to achieve it.

Here Freud can fall back on one of many ad hoc moves, because descriptions of the compulsion to repeat and the death drive have been imprecise, polysemic, and slippery all along. As Zilboorg long ago noted: "The arguments for and against it [the death drive] are of no importance here. What is important is that new concepts, newly formulated, require greater clarity of definition." He added that while individuals are not conscious of the compulsive repetitions, "the compulsive element . . . is not neurotic at all, or not necessarily." It is not more compulsive than breathing. "To use the term 'compulsive' here connotes something that it is not and implies things which are not necessarily there—a rather strange semantic fuzziness on the part of that uniquely clear-minded thinker."[21]

We offer two more instances of Freudian tergiversation in *Beyond the Pleasure Principle.*

First, Freud said, "It is to be noted that only in rare instances can we observe the compulsion to repeat, unsupported by other motives"—i.e., than that of the death drive. Children's play exhibits the compulsion to repeat, but one that is likely in keeping with the pleasure principle and one that is detached from working through (1920, *S.E.*, XVIII: 23).

Second, when examining the precise relationship of the compulsion to repeat to the pleasure principle, Freud stated, "the greater part of what is re-experienced under the compulsion to repeat must cause the ego unpleasure, since it brings to light activities of repressed instinctual impulses." Yet such *Unlust* does not contradict the pleasure principle, as it is, as we have seen, "unpleasure for one system and simultaneously satisfaction for the other" (1920, *S.E.*, XVIII: 20). Moreover, there seems to be a vicious circularity here. The compulsion to repeat is the defining feature of the death drive—"we cannot ascribe to the sexual instinct the characteristic of a compulsion to repeat which first put us on the track of the death instincts" (1920, *S.E.*, XVIII: 56)—hence it cannot be used as an argument for it, which Freud typically does.

Does Freud, then, have in mind certain thresholds of pleasure and unpleasure? What he said immediately hereafter—that there are other past experiences which "include no possibility of pleasure, and which can never, even long ago, have brought satisfaction even to instinctual impulses which have since been repressed"—suggests that thresholds are not in fact the issue (1920, *S.E.*, XVIII: 20).

That is a strong, unestablished claim. Traumatic dreams, for example, through triggering anxiety, call forth defensive efforts to achieve mastery over the anxiety by repressing unconscious material at risk of emergence into consciousness in a way consistent with the pleasure principle. Here traumatic dreams seem to differ nowise, except quantitatively, from the sort of game played by Freud's grandson Ernst, who deliberately engaged himself in an anxiety-laden form of play to master the distressing situation of the disappearance of his beloved mother, save for the brute fact that Ernst enjoyed he game, but the person having a nightmare does not enjoy it. They can be linked to a need to work through material in analysis to achieve consciousness of the unconscious material that triggers the anxiety during these dreams.

Moreover, how is the fact that living things, decaying or expiring, offer evidence of a repetition, and one that is compulsive? It certainly does not seem like a repetition similar to a woman who finds again and again an abusive partner for herself.

Finally, there is Freud's claim in *Beyond the Pleasure Principle* that the compulsion to repeat "seems more primitive, more elementary, more instinctual than the pleasure principle which it over-rides" (1920, *S.E.*, XVIII: 23). He wanted antagonistic drives to explain in some sense certain observable behaviors, certain compulsive repetitions, which he thought were inconsistent with the pleasure principle. Dobson and Katchan find a contradiction. "The assumption of a biological compulsion to repeat earlier states, some of which may elicit unpleasure, seriously contradicts Freud's conceptualization of the pleasure principle—a central tenet of Freud's deterministic psychology. This problem arises because Freud, in order to justify his introduction of the death instinct, had to advocate the primacy of the repetition compulsion over the pleasure principle."[22]

Freud did say, if we follow the lead of Darwin, that sex is not "anything very ancient," as "the extraordinarily violent instincts whose aim it is to bring about sexual union would be repeating something that had once occurred by chance and had since become established [through sexual reproduction] as being advantageous" (1920, *S.E.*, XVIII: 56–57).

Yet that does not give us license to assume "the primacy of the repetition compulsion over the pleasure principle." The evolutionary leap of organic from inorganic must have been driven by some impulse in what is inorganic to become organic—a latent erotic drive or binding force in the inorganic. So too, the tendency of newly formed single-cell organisms to decay or perish was, for Freud, evidence of "*a need to restore an earlier state of things*"—that is, a certain quiescence (1920, *S.E.*, XVIII: 57) in conjunction with the Nirvana Principle—a death drive, again something latent in the inorganic. On this reading, one might say that cellular division, once life first occurred, was in keeping with "*a need to restore an earlier state of things*"—that is, a state of cellular order and quiescence that is not typical of a decadent or moribund cell. Thus, there is no need to maintain that just because something living came out of the inorganic and will return to it that the death drive is primary, or even that there is a death drive. Eros—through the incessant process of cell-division; the strengthening process of conjugation of Protista, weakened by decay, as a form of proto-sexual activity; and the act of sexual reproduction—gains too its victory. When Freud wrote of the death drive as more primitive than Eros—"we may suppose that [the death drive's] final aim is to lead what is living into an inorganic state"[23] (1940, *S.E.*, XXIII: 148)—we need to grant only a sort of axiological primacy, not a temporal primacy, and axiological primacy commits us merely to acknowledgment that what is inorganic temporally precedes what is organic, and that tells us nothing about the nature of the inorganic, which might be infused with impulses toward both life and death.

THE SCIENTIFIC ADEQUACY OF THE DEATH DRIVE

We end with a consideration of the scientific adequacy of Freud's new theory of drives.

In numerous instances, especially when defending himself from critics who question the scientific status of psychoanalysis (e.g., 1925, *S.E.*, XX: 57–58 and 254–57), Freud appealed explicitly to criteria such as fruitfulness, simplicity, and scope. There are several passages concerning the death drive where Freud wrote of the theoretical indispensability of that drive, though there was never any explicit appeal to criteria of scientific adequacy. Yet those passages at least *suggest* that Freud considered his new theory of drives to be simpler, more fruitful, a better fit with the other sciences of his time (especially biology) and with the observable facts, and of greater scope than his old theory of drives.

Freud never undertook a detailed examination of the scientific adequacy of his new theory of drives.[24] In *The Ego and the Id*, where he gave two sustained accounts of the death drive (1923, *S.E.*, XIX: 40–47 and 53–56), he admitted, "In the present discussion . . . I am only putting forward a hypothesis; I have no proof to offer." Thus the lengthy metapsychological description he gave there of how the death drive and Eros function he gave *ex hypothesi*. Freud offered no decisive evidence that the new theory of drives fits the facts better, keeping in mind the old thing was not replete with such evidence either. Moreover, there are no crucial experiments or observations to show, if confirmed, the superiority of the new theory of drives to his old theory of drives. His "hypothesis," without clear-cut examples of predictive consequences, is anything but scientific, but a fortiori, neither was the old theory. He seemed instead, as is often the case when he waxed metapsychologically, to be thinking through things on paper—i.e., showing himself more than his readers that the death drive is not incoherent. Utterances that he cannot do without it perhaps tell us more about Freud's own psychological disposition toward the death drive than about its theoretical indispensability, especially since many future psychoanalysts would do without it.

As we hope to have shown, there is a line of argument that one of us accepts that Freud's old theory of drives seems to accommodate all of his relevant observations better than does the new theory. On this view, the death drive, if anything, added needless complications—how precisely does something acting so silently and unobtrusively interact with Eros, how is the movement from life to death a repetition and a compulsive one, why are not the two drives telic, and how are humans to deal with aggression, if it is the essence of a primitive destructive drive turned outward?

In "Autobiographical Study," however, Freud did address the issue of conceptual fogginess of the death drive. He said: "It remains to be seen whether this construction [the death drive] will turn out serviceable. Although it arose from a desire to fix some of the most important theoretical ideas of psycho-analysis, it goes far beyond psycho-analysis." He then addressed the criticism of the imprecision of "libido" and "drive" and defended his young science with the argument, often used by him, to the effect that no empirical science can begin with precise concepts, for precision comes only with the "progressive analysis of the material of observation." He added, vis-à-vis his metapsychological concepts, "I do not know how far I believe in them" (1925, *S.E.*, XX: 57). That confession was part of an ambivalent attitude Freud would have concerning his new theory of drives till his final days, even though he never returned to his earlier theory.

Defects of the first theory of drives notwithstanding, Holowchak thinks, while Lavin is unsure, that a full examination of the criteria of scientific adequacy (if we are to take these as serviceable barometers of what is scientific), had he expressly undertaken it, would have shown Freud that his new theory of drives was not simpler than the first, that it was anything but fruitful, and that it, because his posit of a death drive went against current biological posits, was not conservative.

The only clear advantage in Freud's new theory of drives is that it seemed to have greater scope in the sense that the death drive is said to be operative in all living things, and seems to fit with his attempt to "biologize" the mind in his unpublished "Project." Another possible advantage is that the new theory allows us to take clinical facts at face value. Without special pleading, there do seem to be plenty of instances where it is hard to believe a patient's behavior is consistent with the pleasure principle. The old theory did seem to require much of what Imre Lakatos once called Monster Barring to retain whatever plausibility it had. Lavin is unashamed of his wondering about what might have been said if Freud had started with the death drive and tried to make a compelling argument for abandoning it in favor of his early theory.

UPSHOT

Why was Freud so committed to the death drive?

There are many possible answers and it may be that all of them contribute something to the etiological picture.

A familiar psychoanalytic answer, endorsed by several[25] in some form or another, is that Freud was driven by internal, unconscious motives of an unpleasant, repetitive nature, with which he himself could not come to terms. In short, his personal psychology—that is, how he internalized his own experiences throughout his life—made the supremacy of the pleasure principle impossible for him to believe.

There were also external factors, to which Freud himself turned to explicate his death-drive commitment, not the least of which were the Great War and the repetitive behaviors exhibited by soldiers,[26] the daemonic and repetitive behaviors of patients in his clinical practice, and certain clinical observations, for instance, the behavior of narcissists, which forced him to modify his metapsychological foundation.[27] Those factors made it difficult for him to believe that there was nothing beyond the pleasure principle.

Furthermore, there was his inflexible commitment to dualism of drives. Human behavior, he consistently believed, was too complex not to be the result of conflicting drives. As psychotherapist Robert Holt wrote, "It was as if [Freud's] conviction about the central importance of conflict forced him always to postulate an opposed duality of basic drives, even if it became necessary to lump together disparate motives with anatomically and physiologically quite separate bases."[28] Preference for Eros and the death drives over ego drives and sex drives occurred because the former allowed not just for conflict, but for antithetical conflict.

By 1920, Freud had become so committed to the death drive that he was willing to incorporate it into his metapsychology—despite the risk of throwing his metapsychology into a state of chaos. So much in the grip of the death drive was Freud that he rejected both the ability of his pre-1920 psychology to accommodate all instances of compulsion to repeat with his old theory of drives and the possibility—one never knows the fate of a theory—that his old theory did not entail the numerous complications of his new theory. As Otto Fenichel's classical exposition argued, it seems that by the time of the structural theory, Freud's reliance on repetition compulsion lost its rationale.[29]

NOTES

1. Still, Lavin thinks this much is plain. Nobody would cite nightmares, masochistic beatings, fetishistic coprophagia as exemplars of the pleasure principle or to teach it to somebody who did not know about it. In fact, in philosophical discussion, one might offer these as counterexamples to the pleasure principle. As for child's play, the use of play to reduce a child's anxiety is very well known. Children also play contact sports that have a degree of pain built into them. Play does though help a child attain a level of mastery over the kinds of problems confronted in a child's life.

2. Play, as used in child analysis, may also involve working through.

3. An alternative is to view Freud as having concluded, based on his clinical work, that the new theory of drives permitted a better organization and comprehension of the clinical, but he was not content to rest his case on that alone. He supplemented this inference to a best

explanation with biological arguments that, echoing the late Peters Strawson, amount to "a non sequitur of numbing grossness."

4. Peter D. Kramer, *Freud* (New York: HarperCollins, 2006), 167.

5. Freud would not see himself as making this silly mistake. He already thought he needed a dualism. He changed an already dualistic account to accommodate the clinical data. He then provided a variety of arguments for doing so. Lavin thinks lot of social science is done without arguing for a set of constructs. You use them, and see how they work. For example, in speaking of IQ tests, long custom speaks of crystallized and fluid intelligence. The distinction is not forced. A standard IQ test like Wechsler's thought to have subtests that focus on crystallized intelligence (viz., vocabulary) and fluid intelligence (viz., Block Design). Much of the argument for these constructs emerges after the Principal Component Analysis has been done and the factor named. Sometimes it works out, sometimes it does not. One is not even committed to saying alternative sets of factors or constructs to describe the results are wrong.

6. Peter D. Kramer, *Freud*, 168.

7. David H. Wolpert, "Information Width: A Way for the Second Law to Increase Complexity," ed. Charles H. Lineweaver, Paul C. W. Davies, and Michael Ruse (Cambridge: Cambridge University Press, 2013), 249.

8. Paul Davies, "Directional Principles from Cancer to Cosmology," ed. Charles H. Lineweaver, Paul C. W. Davies, and Michael Ruse (Cambridge: Cambridge University Press, 2013), 30.

9. John Maynard Smith and Eörs Száthmary, *Major Transitions in Evolution* (Oxford: Oxford University Press, 1995), 3.

10. Börgje Ekstig, "Complexity, Natural Selection and the Evolution of Life and Humans," https://link.springer.com/article/10.1007/s10699-014-9358-y, accessed 12 April 2017.

11. Martin Seligman, *Authentic Happiness: Using the New Positive Psychology to Realize Your Potential for Lasting Fulfillment* (New York: Free Press, 2002), 258.

12. Martin Seligman, *Authentic Happiness*, 260.

13. C. Schmidt-Hellerau, "Libido and Lethe: Fundamentals of Formalised Conception of Metapsychology," *International Journal of Psycho-Analysis*, 1997, 691.

14. Edward Bibring, "The Development and Problems of the Theory of Instincts," *International Journal of Psychoanalysis*, vol. 50, 306.

15. Research however does suggest a link between sex and aggression. The amygdala (the part of the brain believed responsible for aggression) and the hypothalamus (the part of the brain that regulates aggression and that is responsible for emotive activity) are close to each other and excitation of the one generally is excitation of the other. See Robert Sapolesky, "Testosterone Rules," *Discover* vol. 18, no. 3, 45–50, and Gene Bylinsky, "New Clues to the Causes of Violence," *Fortune*, January, 1973, 135.

16. Social scientists may find some of this argument perplexing. Is the alleged existence of a behavioral account of a psychoanalytic phenomenon proof that the psychoanalytic phenomenon is not really psychoanalytic? If I say that the kidneys remove contaminants from blood, does the existence of people with kidney disease a refutation? If I say *smoking causes cancer*, am I refuted, as cigarette makers would like, if I produce healthy, long-lived smokers? One of us reads these kinds of passages as Freud treating his new theory as the type of device he claims it to be. Had he not thought of it, he may well have stuck with the special pleading its use would require. One of us wishes that he had so stuck.

17. Edward Bibring, "The Development and Problems of the Theory of Instincts," *International Journal of Psychoanalysis*, vol. 50, 306.

18. The lexical definition of "compulsion" is in fact the wrong one. In clinical psychology, is, in the paradigmatic case, used to reduce the anxiety created by an obsession. In this sense, if put in behavioral terms, a behavior that is negatively reinforced. The behavior appears because something undesired goes away. The behavior does not create pleasure. Taking aspirin is negatively reinforced. Something unwanted, pain, goes away after taking it. There is no aspirin buzz.

19. M. Dobson and O. Katchan, "Freud's Concept of the Death Instinct: Is It a Logical Construct?" *Australian Journal of Psychotherapy*, vol. 11, no. 1, 1992, 62–63.

20. This passage should be read with caution regarding future developments as its use of anxiety pre-dates Freud's recognition of signal anxiety.

21. Gregory Zilboorg, "Introduction, in Sigmund Freud, *Beyond the Pleasure Principle* (New York: W.W. Norton & Company, 1961), xxxiii–xxxiv.

22. M. Dobson and O. Katchan, "Freud's Concept of the Death Instinct," 66. This argument itself represents an extreme privileging of the Pleasure Principle

23. Recall also in *Beyond the Pleasure Principle*, where he writes of the death drive's function as "the most universal endeavour of all living substance" (1920, *S.E.*, XVIII: 62).

24. Scientific adequacy, for Lavin, is a dark term of art. Freudian psychoanalysis was a science. He hoped it would cohere well with other sciences; however, his final theory of drives was intended to aid psychoanalytic, not biological, science. The idea of arranging elements in terms of their scientific number is central in elementary chemistry, and yet it has no obvious role in psychoanalysis or biology. Holowchak thinks otherwise.

25. André Green, "The Repetition Compulsion," *Psychoanalytic Review*, vol. 69, no. 4, 1982/1983, 455–69; 1982/1983; Ernest Jones, *The Life and Work of Sigmund Freud: Vol. 3. The Last Phase, 1919–1939* (New York: Basic Books, 1957); M. Schur, *Freud: Living and Dying* (New York: International Universities Press, 1972); and Lawrence Kubie, "A Critical Analysis of the Concept of a Repetition Compulsion," *International Journal of Psycho-Analysis*, 20, 1969, 390–402.; P. E. Stepansky, "A History of Aggression," *Psychological Issues* (Monograph 39, New York: International Universities Press, 1977); and Peter D. Kramer, *Freud* (New York: HarperCollins, 2006), 168–69.

26. E. Schwartz and J. T. Peterfreund, *Information, Systems, and Psychoanalysis* (New York: International University Press, 1971).

27. Says Lind, "How fundamentally incognito the death drive remained to Freud's mind is perhaps also indicated by his inability or unwillingless to give a definite name to it" (1991, 72–3).

28. Robert Holt, *Freud Reappraised: A Fresh Look at Psychoanalytic Theory* (New York: The Guilford Press, 1989), 179.

29. Otto Fenichel, *Psychoanalytic Theory of Neurosis*, 50th Anniversary Edition (New York: W.W. Norton and Company, 1995), 58–61 and 129–31. One reason for this is that the structural theory, the signal theory of anxiety, and the resultant picture of the mind as an arena of perpetual conflict led to an emphasis on defense mechanisms, rather than the interpretations of unconscious content that marked early psychoanalysis. Oddly, the analysts most willing to accept the death instinct, the Kleinians, retained the practice of interpreting content to an extent much stronger than that favored by the classical psychoanalysis championed by Anna Freud, with its focus on defense interpretation.

Chapter Seven

The Future of Psychotherapy

Our project has been undertaken for both critical and historical reasons. We have aimed to understand Freud. Just what is the compulsion to repeat and does it provide evidence of some primal drive that points beyond the pleasure principle? Moreover, how did Freud arrive at his notion of a compulsion to repeat? Finally, just what is salvageable?

To answer such questions, we historically take what might seem to be an twisted path. We begin in part 1 with a study of the uses, both clinical and phylogenetic, to which Freud put the concept of repetition, and we find a multiplicity of uses. In part 2, we turn to the development of the compulsion to repeat first as a clinical concept and then, years later, as a seemingly indispensable metapsychological concept.

This third part is critical. We begin in the prior chapter with an investigation of Freud's resolution concerning the death drive. In this chapter, the focus is on salvaging what can be salvaged of both repetition and the theory of drives. We begin with the mysterious nature of "drive." We then turn to attempts by psychotherapists to vindicate Freud. All such attempts, we maintain, are inconclusive, as the complications of introduction of a destructive drive yield less accommodating certain problematic observations—such as repetitive traumatic dreams and narcissistic behavior—to the theory of ego drives and sex drives. Our assessment of the death drive made, we continue by arguing that "repetition" and "compulsion to repeat" are worthy of psychological consideration on their own. Analyzing the secondary literature on the two concepts, we give readers a taste of different employments of the two concepts for a future of psychotherapy.

THE NATURE OF "TRIEB"

We begin this chapter with a brief discussion of a preliminary problem—the inferential "justification" of the concept of drive.

Allan Compton argues that there is a three-step process to arrive at drives. Freud begins with the elements of consciousness and assumes all persons have a similar conscious awareness. Next, because of the instability of consciousness, we infer unconscious phenomena, characterized by mostly sexual urges. Last, we infer a somatic source of unconscious phenomena. "An instinctual drive is thus an explanatory construct and one which depends upon the inference of unconscious mental processes."[1] In such a manner, Freud, according to Compton, feels the need to go etiologically beyond the unconscious in some effort to ground psychological posits in biology. The difficulty here is that the inference from step 1 to step 2—viz., to the existence of unconscious phenomena in the unique Freudian manner—is sufficiently problematic. The inference to drives, undergirding those unconscious phenomena and only indirectly observed, is even more problematic. Overall, the worth of "drive" as an explanatory construct is only as sound as the work that it does.

Here again Compton offers us another problem vis-à-vis drives: "They can readily explain too much." Freud, as we have seen, was wedded to the notion of two drives, but left open the question of the number of drives subsumable under each drive. "Circumscription of the number of drives then becomes essential if the concept is to be useful or even meaningful."[2]

It is this "frontier" nature of drive—that "observational data are primarily psychological [while] a core concept [of drive] has a central somatic referent [that leads to] build in ambiguity in mind-body terms"—that is problematic.[3] That is why some psychotherapists have chosen to strip *Trieb* of any biological reference.[4]

VINDICATING FREUD

Freud was not shy about acknowledging that his view of a death drive was Schopenhauerian. "You may perhaps shrug your shoulders and say: 'That isn't natural science, it's philosophical philosophy!' But, ladies and gentlemen, why should not a bold thinker have guessed something that is afterwards confirmed by sober and painstaking detailed research?'" (1932, *S.E.*, XXII: 107) Yet Freud went on to say that he had transcended Schopenhauer in positing two drives: a death drive and a sex drive.

Has the death drive been confirmed "by sober and painstaking detailed research" or have data merely been fitted to the theory?

There has been no greater acceptance of Freud's life and death drives than in the work of Melanie Klein. People have a powerful fear of annihilation, generated by fear of death, indicative of a drive. Infants, through nurture, begin by forming a close bond with their mother, who fulfills immediate needs. When needs are unmet, infants feel anxiety and frustration, and there arise aggressive impulses. "The anxiety evoked in the child by his destructive impulses takes effect in two ways. In the first place it makes him afraid of being exterminated himself by those very impulses, i.e., it relates to an internal instinctual danger; and in the second place, it focuses his fears on his external object, against whom his sadistic feelings are directed as a source of danger."[5] The young ego assumes a defensive posture. "The excess of sadism [aggression] gives rise to anxiety and sets in motion the ego's earliest mechanisms of defence."[6]

Edward Bibring, in addressing the issue of lack of clinical relevance for the death drive, argued that "the theory was not set up on the grounds of any fresh psychological material or indeed of any question of a psychological nature; it was the result of certain theoretical problems which had been raised by previous hypotheses and which it was designed to solve." The theory of drives is biology-driven, not psychology-driven.[7] He added: "Instincts of life and death are not psychologically perceptible as such: they are biological instincts whose existence is required by hypothesis alone." It follows that "the theory of primal instincts is a concept which ought only to be adduced in a theoretical context and not in discussions of a clinical or empirical character." Along those biological lines, the questions concern whether death occurs by "an injury from without" or "life has a natural end." If the latter, then there is justification for positing a death drive.[8]

Against the view that there are other motives for human behavior (e.g., those outlined by Carl Rogers), Bibring smartly noted that drives for Freud "were not thought of as directing the whole course of mental events, but only as being sources of energy and causes of excitation which set in motion the regulative trends of the mental apparatus."[9]

R. J. Bocock sees no difficulty in the shift from the early to the later theory of drives. "The change was necessitated by the need to be rational, as well as by the data of analysis itself." The rational problem "was that there was no clear opposition between sexual and ego instincts, that the two fused into one another too much for them to work as an opposed pair of instincts." If the ego could be the object of the sex drive, then there was no need for Freud to posit two separate drives. Moreover, there were certain observations that the first theory of drives could not accommodate, though he says queerly "observations only [are] made possible by the use of the concepts"—a stark admission that there can be no "atomic" facts.[10] Facts for Bocock are not neutral, but "are generated by conceptual system and methods which the different sciences employ," and "the later instinct theory is more rational and consistent given the other concepts of psychoanalysis, than the other instinct theory formulations."[11]

Jacques Lacan, like Freud, believed the death drive is a substratal concept of psychoanalysis. Yet there are two dissimilarities. First, for Lacan, it is not biological,[12] as it is for Freud. Early on, associated with the pre-oedipal phase of psychological development and linked with the suicidal tendency of narcissism, it is thought to be part of the "imaginary order." Upon later developing his view of the imaginary, symbolic, and real, the death drive is now part of the symbolic, not the imaginary, as it is the "mask of the symbolic order."[13] Second, it is not a drive that is antipodal to the sexual drives as it is for Freud, but an element of all drives. Lacan claimed, "Every drive is virtually a death drive," since every drive aims at its own extinction, embroils all persons in repetition, and extends beyond the pleasure principle, where pleasure is experienced as pain.[14] This excess of enjoyment (*jouissance*) is a repetitive return to transgression of the pleasure principle and aims at death.[15] Thus, for Lacan, the death drive assumes a primacy that it did not have even for Freud.

André Green was a pupil of Lacan and is also interested in preserving the death drive in psychoanalysis, though he is, as we may remember, critical of Freud's explication of the interplay of Eros and the death drive. For Green, the death drive is an "inclination to self-disappearance" that is through a "disobjectualizing function" (a process by which a person becomes "any object" or even "no object at all."[16] Thus the death drive, which functions "for the most part, on the side of repetition," is coupled more to nothingness than to aggression or destructiveness. The negativity of the death drive is linked with "catastrophic or unthinkable anxieties" and dread of annihilation, breakdown, futility, devitalization, and psychic death, as well as sensations of a gap, bottomless holes, or abysses. He claimed: "If the repetition compulsion is daemonic, it appears to be due to its narcissistic nature which is bound endlessly to repeat itself. The pleasure principle stems from an evolution in the object's response and it may ultimately become inexorable, losing its quality to safeguard us, to act as guardian of our survival and end up being an ally of the repetition compulsion. But, by and large, it acts on the side of Eros to preserve our life and to fight against the destructive drives occurring, for the most part, on the side of repetition."[17]

Michel de M'Uzan is yet another French analyst who aims to preserve drive theory, without a death drive. He posits, however, only the sexual drives, which naturally terminate in death. Each person has a "life programme" that leads to self-extinction. The life programme functions through developmental stages to mature and protect each person, but it also has a "preordained finiteness." It follows that he has no need of a "special drive, the so-called death drive."[18] In a manner of speaking, "one dies after having finished living."[19]

What however about the relation between compulsion to repeat and the drives? The customary conjunction between compulsion to repeat and the death drive, he asserts, has been responsible for numerous difficulties. *Pace* Freud, no repetition is "perpetual recurrence of the same thing." For the most part, each repetition is an altered version of what has been announced previously.[20] Repetitions of the identical are special repetitions, which need not be explicated by reference to a death instinct; they are merely indications of a certain type of organization that "forms part of an individual's development,"[21] "never has a really fatal nature" in neurotics, and rarely completely restricts a subject's capacity to choose.[22]

Jean Laplanche, an analyst and coauthor of an esteemed dictionary of psychoanalytic terms, maintains that we can salvage Freud's drive theory if we impose the following restrictions. First, we must dismiss any notion of the life drive and the death drive as biological concepts. Second, life drives and death drives are uniquely human. Third, the two drives are not oppositional—it is not a "difference between sexuality and a non-sexual aggressivity"—but both are sexual drives: the sexual life drives are secondary binding forces and the sexual death drives are primary unbinding forces. Finally, the two drives only loosely correspond to the topographical difference between the ego and the id, as most but not all of the ego's processes are bound and most but not all of the id's processes are unbound.[23]

According to Richard Wollheim, Freud has two broad classes of repetition. On the one hand, there are repetitions that enable the psychical apparatus to continue to work over and even master prior representations of a person's experience. This work is congruent with the pleasure principle. On the other hand, Wollheim, a philosopher whose influences include Kleinian psychoanalysis, took it that Freud thought some repetitions go to such an extreme that the psychical apparatus in relation to them is brought to an early psychical state that is profoundly primitive, and in the idealized case, empty of energy. This state of zero energy would be a death state and one "beyond the pleasure principle."[24]

On Wollheim's reading, this conjecture of Freud links the death drive to Freud's Nirvana Principle. It also, in its emphasis on the defensive move to a profoundly preverbal psychological position, resonates with the work of Fred Bush (discussed below), and of course, with modern Kleinians.

What is to be said concerning such attempts to vindicate Freud?

Many analysts may well have sympathy for the idea that their patients do exhibit two conflicting and antipodal "drives." On one hand, there is a force that favors greater integration and consciousness. It is a force that favors "adult" solutions to life's riddles. On the other hand, some analysts think it is useful to have a way of conceptualizing another force that is marked in the life of some patients, especially for example, patients with high levels of psychopathology. These patients do make psychic retreats to profoundly empty levels of consciousness. To be with them in counter-transference is a personally annihilating, emptying experience—one that makes work with these persons an extremely technical and personal challenge. Yet it is work that also requires some comprehension of the allure of death and of nothingness, especially when integrated solutions to a deep-rooted psychical problem seem beyond reach.

To acknowledge that something like a death drive sometimes seems theoretically helpful, however, is not to acknowledge its theoretical indispensability, its existence in all persons, or even its heuristic merit. Freud's evidence for a death drive is only loosely empirical. He adduces arguments in favor of the "daemonic" sense of repetitive phenomena and the death drive, while he ignores and fails to address the numerous cogent criticisms of both. He repeatedly says that the death drive is mostly silent, unobtrusive, and that perhaps gives him the latitude to posit it in order to solve certain conceptual problems without having to say much about it.[25]

ABANDONING THE DEATH DRIVE

There is a large body of critical literature concerning Freud's shift to his new theory of drives. Most of that literature argues that the move was a mistake. The problems that posed challenges to his old theory of drives were not irreconcilable with the old theory—at least, not without some conceptual reshuffling, as it were. We offer merely a small sample from that literature.

For Allan Compton, there is the problem of aggression, the defining characteristic of the death drive. What data show aggression to be a drive? How does the death drive explain the data? What is the precise relationship between the aggressive death drive and Eros?

Following Compton, there are simple and complex bodily sensations. The former include the special senses, and each is related to specific end-organs and nerve fibers with "well-traced pathways through the spinal cord and brain stem." The more complex include hunger, thirst, need to urinate or defecate, urges to sneeze or yawn, and sexual sensations. Both groups can be straightforwardly linked with pleasure and pain through sensory excitation or withdrawal of what is sensibly painful.[26] This is the biological picture, according to Compton, from which Freud drew for his first theory of drives.

"None of these considerations of sensations of somatic tension/relief and subjective distress/pleasure apply to 'aggression.'" Aggression is biologically linked with the fight/flight sequence in preparation for action, but it cannot be cashed out so easily in psychoanalytic terms as for instance can sexual motives. Sexual motives arise internally; aggression seems to be triggered by external stimuli.[27] Moreover, when they are thus cashed out, they are cashed out in language eerily similar to sexual etiology. "Aggressive elements (ideas, feelings, impulses)," continues Compton, "seem to be mentally similar to sexual elements: they are warded off and are a source of mental conflict." He sums up, "We thus arrive at the conclusion that the psychoanalytic clinical evidence for aggression as a drive is, in this respect, very similar to the evidence for sexual drives, while the background of supporting, physiologic, and directly observable evidence present for sexuality is totally absent for aggression."[28] What then is the warrant for aggression as a drive?

André Green takes issue with Freud's change of theories. "It was in fact a very perilous decision to give up the sovereignty of the pleasure principle, because opening the way to the destructive drives reinforced the repetition compulsion."[29] Freud wished for antagonistic drives, but he also sometimes wrote of the compulsion to repeat and "instinctual satisfaction which is immediately pleasurable" as forming "an intimate relationship" (1920, *S.E.*, XVIII: 23).

Maintaining with Freud that any metapsychological explanation "must be constrained by neurobiology," Brian Johnson looks to neuro-psychoanalysis, in a nonreductionist manner, to vindicate Freud's posit of a death drive. He begins by defining neuroscientifically Freud's "metapsychological concept of drive" as "activity in the ventral tegmental dopaminergic SEEKING disposition, independent of world events," which is characterized not by "pleasure of satisfaction," but by "enthusiastic positive excitement, interest, desire, and euphoria." Thus the urge for cocaine, which addicts often use though they dislike the way it makes them feel, trumping the urge for pizza can be explicated. "Cocaine induces an artificial drive by blocking the dopamine reuptake transporter protein, resulting in much-increased stimulation of nucleus accumbens neurons." After "repeated exposure" to cocaine, the brain becomes reorganized, and one hungry for pizza will choose cocaine if each is readily available.[30]

Yet even the destructive behavior of cocaine-seeking is easily explicable by the drive for pleasure. "The difference between emotional health and neurosis is that happiness is a byproduct of functioning well; the drive system and the pleasure system line up seamlessly." He continues: "There is nothing 'compulsive' about the repetition compulsion. What Freud had been observing in the transference was the eternal conflict between pleasure and the drive to recreate remembered relationships or previously pleasurable fantasies." According to Johnson: "Occam's razor dispenses with the death instinct—no need to create an explanation that is already elegantly and parsimoniously explained by metapsychological concepts of drive, pleasure, and cathexis that are well supported by neuroscience research." Thus "'repetition compulsion' and 'death instinct' were created to fix a problem that . . . never existed."[31]

Nicole Kirman, whose elegant summary of the transformation of the compulsion to repeat from clinical to metapsychological concept we recapitulated at the end of chapter 4, argues that the "contradictions, confusions and controversies" concerning the compulsion to repeat occur because of its ascendancy as a metapsychological concept and its link to the death drive. She states that it is best to put aside all metapsychological discussion of *Wiederholungszwang*—"it is not only not an expression of a death drive, but . . . it is an attempt to reaffirm one's psychic existence, one's self at a core level"—and focus on its relevance as a clinical concept. She claims, "The repetition compulsion refers to what is being enacted rather than remembered; it is part of the individual's character; it does not include every repetition, but is limited to the repetition of painful experiences; it appears in the transference; it is distinguished by its intractable resistance to treatment."[32]

Yet that separation is precisely a move that Cordelia Schmidt-Hellerau forbids. "The clinical facts we establish and their formulation are thus never entirely independent of theory." She bids us to reexamine the Freudian metapsychological scaffolding and check it for consistency.[33]

When she turns to Freud's introduction of the death drive in 1920, she notes, as we have earlier, that the process of "*pressure and repression*" is a repetition. "From this point of view the compulsion to repeat would not be confined to the repressed, the unconscious, but should be seen as a property inherent in all systems of the psychical apparatus. . . . In other words, *the compulsion to repeat is a structural phenomenon*." Yet that is at odds with Freud's prior conception of a drive as "a factor impelling towards change and development." It is now a principle of conservation, and that principle is characteristic of "the *structural* situation of the system and not the drive element in itself." That returns us to the telic problem, covered in the chapter prior. Schmidt-Hellerau ends with some comments on human aggression as indicative of a primary drive or as "*affect* or *affective action*." Her preference is the latter.[34] There is no need to adopt a death drive.

Finally, Norman Lear—attending to Freud's lengthy argument which culminates in the conclusion, "*The aim of all life is death*"—argues that the problem is merely a focus on repetition. "It is not just that his solution to the problem is invalid; he is not clear about what the problem is. He focuses on repetition; but, in my opinion, the new and puzzling phenomenon he discovered is the mind's active disruption of its own functioning." He adds, "Freud's question was 'Why does the mind aim at repetition?'; it ought to have been 'Why and how does the mind disrupt itself?'"[35]

COMPULSION TO REPEAT AND HUMAN MENTATION

Where now do we go?

As we have shown, Freud discovered that repetition was an axial concept of psychoanalysis—perhaps, as we have said, *the* axial concept of psychoanalysis—and has shown that it is a needed concept in psychoanalytic understanding of neurosis and that it plays a significant role in therapy itself. Moreover, his study of psychopathological behavior showed that certain repetitions—the repetitive dreams of traumatized soldiers, the in-clinic behaviors of highly repressed patients, the avoidance behavior of phobics, and the "rituals" of obsessive-compulsives—were of the compulsive sort. Such findings can neither be ignored nor should they be abandoned.

The most promising line of research, we maintain, is that of freeing completely "repetition" and "compulsion to repeat" from any mysterious connection to "an urge inherent in organic life to restore an earlier [quiescent] state of things." Repetition and compulsion to repeat, as they relate to human pathology, are worth analysis in their own right, as those phenomena, at least, have empirical warrant in Freud's groundbreaking work on psychopathology. Also, as we have shown by our chosen examples, there is no agreed current notion of what the death instinct is.

Many researchers in various disciplines are doing just that. They are seeking greater conceptual clarification of "repetition" and "compulsion to repeat" through more refined observations of the sorts of repetitions, pathological and otherwise, humans exhibit. Our focus prohibits an attempt at anything like an exhaustive account at the numerous contributors, following in Freud's footsteps, who are making sizeable contributions in research on memory and psychopathology. This section offers a small sample of that research, focusing on repetition or compulsion to repeat as it relates to human memory.

That the notion of repetition is fundamental to mental development and proper functioning was apparent to one of the pioneers on human cognitive development—Jean Piaget. For Piaget, mental structures, essentially dynamic, function according to operational rules and the system as a whole seeks equilibrium. Children begin with reflex behaviors—such as thumb sucking—the basic property of which is repetition. Through repetition, the sucking reflex is reproductively assimilated to other objects—from sucking his fingers, a child sucks others' fingers within his grasp, his pillow, his quilt, and his bedclothes. Piaget inferred, "Consequently he assimilates these objects to the activity of the reflex." Overall, repetition enables children to incorporate other objects into their "schemata" and eventually differentiate among them—thereby refining the schemata.[36]

Daniel Juda uses a Piagetian perspective to understand how the compulsion to repeat, over time, relates to cognitive development. "The repetition compulsion is the *sine qua non* of adaptation, of development, of the maturational process, and if anything, a stubborn persistence in man to attempt to assimilate and accommodate reality (although sometimes a relatively inadequate attempt)." *Pace* Freud, there is no attempt to deny the external world. "Instead, the repetition compulsion is an attempt to mull over difficult and poorly understood problems." Repetition occurs compulsively because certain data threaten to disrupt our schemata—that is, they cannot be easily accommodated. Failure to compulsively repeat sometimes can be life-threatening.[37] Thus, there is no pressing need to concern ourselves with the adequacy of drive theory.

Psychoanalyst Joseph Lichtenberg, based on his own research on repetitions in infant development, offers an alternative to Freud's high-tension state experiences. For Freud, state experiences, whether trauma-driven or the result of somato-erotic zonal excitement, are comparable to the disruptive effect of a rock thrown into a placid pond. Lichtenberg, in contrast, recognizes "low and moderate-tension state experiences," in which redundancies—"repetitious action patternings of infant and caretaker"—occur. Here the rock-in-the-pond analogy falters, as the pond, symbolizing the infant in a milieu—such as exchanges between an infant and his mother—is recognized to be not in the least placid. An infant in a milieu makes up "an extremely complex ecological system with continuous change occurring in multiple subsystems (chemical, biological, diurnal, and evolutionary)." For illustration, an infant's response of cooing, clucking, and smiling on seeing his mother can only be understood against the "background of a structured interaction, built out of repetition and expectancy."[38] Later, Lichtenberg compares the repetitions in exchanges between analyst and patient with those repetitions between mother and child. In therapy, an analyst-patient exchange builds "background expectations" for therapeutic progress. Here the basic patterns of repetitions and expectancies are not altered to mold behavior, but analyzed so that their meaning becomes clear. In mothering, the mother-infant exchange is altered by the mother to promote growth and independence.[39] The influence of Freud in both instances is readily recognizable.

A. H. Modell, attending to the work of G. Edelman on memory, states that memory is dynamic, not static. He refers back to a letter (Freud to Fleiss), where Freud spoke of *Nachträglichkeit* or deferred action as involving memory as a "retranscription." Memory, Freud noted, is something that is continually reshaped to meet present action. Modell states, "*The compulsion to repeat represents a compulsion to seek a perceptual identity between present and past objects.*" Thus, it offers clues to a solution to the paradox of how repetition can give rise to new experiences. Freud's transference neurosis may be linked with the notion of memory as perceptual recategorization. Transference, as it involves repetition of painful experiences, may be a research for perceptual categories that transcends the pleasure principle.[40]

Finally, Hans Jürgen Wirth says that the compulsion to repeat characterizes, in a negative sense, the creative person who sees the imperfection of his work and is doomed to rework it ad nauseum. It may also characterize, in a positive sense, the possibility of new experiences. "Every repetition contains the possibility of new perspectives opening up through minute variations of the repeated fundamental conflict. Every repetition presents the attempt of revision and the further development of the original pattern of conflict. . . . From this perspective, repetition is a creative act that allows something unfinished to be seen again in a creative light."[41]

PATHOLOGICAL SENSES

There are, of course, psychopathological senses of repetition and compulsion to repeat.

Psychoanalyst Fred Bush argues that the compulsion to repeat expresses itself as a comprehensible recurrent defense during the course of an analysis. To understand its defensive aim, a therapist and patient must conceive of the patient's relevant repetitive behavior that is often disguised as an "action-thought." Action-thoughts are polysemous remnants of earlier compromise formations. To analyze repetitions, an analyst must keep in mind that a repetition is not an undisguised action from early childhood. Instead, it is a "complex series of reactions expressed in a type of thinking prevalent at the time the conflict first appeared."[42]

The therapist and patient must absorb four lessons to make sense of the patient's compulsion to repeat. First, the patient's compulsion to repeat expresses an archaic solution to a riddle from the patient's childhood. The compulsion to repeat expresses a child's early nonlinguistic solution to a behavioral challenge during his childhood. Second, a repetition manages to establish itself as a preeminent solution to the child's challenge because of the lengthy time a child has to rely on nonlinguistic solutions to life's riddles. Third, the solution is disguised from the patient because it is an archaic, pre-linguistic solution, in the context of adulthood, which is neurotic because an adult has the resources to achieve a better solution and to make the whole process conscious through words. Finally, while repetitions are unanalyzed, their defensive purpose remains hidden because the old conflict it "solves" is only partially solved. In short, a compulsion to repeat is a partial, pre-linguistic solution to a childhood conflict.[43]

Because the conflict is only partially resolved, it continues to find expression in a patient's daily life, albeit now in the form of an "action thought." This defensive solution is tenacious and invisible because of being over-learned—the patient has relied on it in one disguise or another for many years—and does temporarily reduce signal anxiety when employed. The price of a partial solution is that the unconscious material against which the repetition defends remains unconscious to the patient and the conflict never yields to a complete solution.[44]

Psychoanalyst Robert Shapiro, following Freud's lead in his watershed work "Remembering, Repeating, and Working-Through" (1914), takes repetitions as behaviors that express a need to reunite with parental figures—especially in times of stress. "The anxiety generated by actions or feelings that symbolically indicate movement away from the parents is particularly likely to stimulate repetitions that rekindle the early parent-child relationship." He adds, "This need is rooted in disturbances in the separation-individuation process."[45] By focusing on such repetitions in therapy, an analyst gains clues to the conflicted nature of early parental attachments.

Arnold Wilson and Carol Malatesta propose that there are two types of repetition, primal and symbolic, and that the compulsion to repeat is a "motivational explanation" for the former only. Primal repetition originates early in human development and contains the actual dyadic interaction between caregiver and child. It is less influenced by time and occurs during preverbal and presymbolic development. Thus, its causes are beyond the reach of "verbal and memorial access" and analysts must be in the position to interpret repetitions without verbal and symbolic cues.[46]

In his paper "The Uses of Repetition," Paul Libbey Russell attempts at disambiguation of the compulsion to repeat. "The repetition compulsion would seem to be two things. One is the nucleus of an organized system of affective incompetence, a dysfunctional feeling system. It is also an attempt to continue an interrupted relationship in the service of the emotional growth that was earlier broken off. It is the scar tissue of the injury to the capacity to feel." As such, it is an attachment to the past that destroys the present and the person. In therapy, there is genuine risk. An analyst attempts to make the analytic situation "enough like the past to virtually insure [*sic*] a repetition of an emotionally crippling loss." There is also the possibility of a "negotiation for feeling an attachment in the service of growth."[47]

Roderick Ørner and Peter Stolz address the assumed homogeneity of repetitive phenomena in psychotherapy and psychotraumatology. They are developing a viable empirical approach that synthesizes the speculations of psychoanalysis with the latest empirical research in biology. They focus on the use of dreams as a "prototype repetition," and argue that the phenomenological diversity of repetition in dreams is consistent with repetition in cognitive studies.[48]

UPSHOT

How are we to end such a book, which has taken us on a fantastic empirical and theoretical journey?

We begin with some comments on Freud's theories of drives. At this point, Holowchak draws two conclusions. First, there is at least heuristic merit in Freud's posit of his early theory of drives that does not exist in his later theory, which showcases the mostly silent, but largely dominant death drives. Second, Freud should never have abandoned the ego drives and sex drives. The new theory, though offering simpler solutions to problems such as narcissism and human aggression, introduced large complexities concerning the interactions of Eros and the death drives that Freud never fully explicated, because he never had much to say about what precisely the death drive does, about how the death drive interacts with Eros, and about the number and types of particular drives under Eros and the death drive.[49] The result was irremediable conceptual confusion.

Lavin, in contrast, concludes that drive theory is a perspective, but one that must be used with caution. The early drive theory is, like senate committees of old, defunct. It is no more than a historical curiosity. To the extent clinicians use drive theory, they use Freud's theory of affiliative and destructive drives, but as readers will have noticed, without any deep agreements about how to specify the theory. He also found himself suspicious of, even hostile to, the status of the Pleasure Principle as our work progressed.

Still, whatever our disagreements, we must acknowledge that the journey that Freud took to get "beyond the pleasure principle" was remarkable. That it ended by him taking a controverted turn in 1920 ought to be of no great consequence to us. The mistake was honest.

We turn now to "repetition" and the "compulsion to repeat."

What researchers in this chapter have shown is that, while the notion of a death drive may have been infertile, "repetition" and "compulsion to repeat" have led to much fruitful research at the empirical and conceptual levels by psychoanalysts, biologists, cognitive psychologists, and even philosophers.

And so, while there is a pronounced tendency in the literature to denigrate Freud either for supplanting his old theory of drives with his new one or for introduction of drive theory in the first place, there has been little praise for Freud's recognition that repetitions are invaluable assets in clinical therapy and in research into human cognitive development—especially mnemonic research. This book is in some measure an attempt to remedy that defect and give Freud the recognition that is due to him.

Few scientists are much noticed in a lifetime for their efforts. Fewer scientists when wrong are noticed at all. Yet there is a difference between being wrong outright and being interestingly wrong. Freud, having taken a wrong turn, and that is the majority opinion, in *Beyond the Pleasure Principle*, wound up at least being interestingly wrong, because the path he blazed in his focus on repetition in human behavior had numerous remarkable twists and turns that have led today to extraordinary and plethoric research in human cognition and psychopathology. For such things, we have Freud to thank.

NOTES

1. Allan Compton, "The Current Status of the Psychoanalytic Theory of Instinctual Drives," *Psychoanalytic Quarterly*, vol. 52, 1983, 367.
2. Allan Compton, "The Current Status of the Psychoanalytic Theory of Instinctual Drives," 379
3. Allan Compton, "The Current Status of the Psychoanalytic Theory of Instinctual Drives," 366.
4. E.g., Charles Brenner, *An Elementary Textbook of Psychoanalysis* (New York: International University Press, 1955), 16–17; Hans W. Loewald, "On Motivation and Instinct Theory," *Psychoanalytical Study of the Child*, vol. 26, 1971, 105; and R. J. Stoller, *Sexual Excitement: Dynamics of Erotic Life* (New York: Pantheon), 1979, 6–7.
5. Melanie Klein, "The Early Stages of the Oedipus Conflict and of Super-Ego Formation," *The Psychoanalysis of Children* (London: The Hogarth Press, 1933), 184.
6. Melanie Klein, "The Importance of Symbol Formation in Ego Development," *The Selected Melanie Klein*, ed. J. Mitchell (London: Penguin Books, 1986), 96.
7. See also Erich Fromm, *The Crisis of Psycho-Analysis* (Greenwich, CT: Fawcett Books, 1970), 46–47.
8. Edward Bibring, "The Development and Problems of the Theory of Instincts," *International Journal of Psychoanalysis*, vol. 50, 1969, 301–3.
9. Edward Bibring, "The Development and Problems of the Theory of Instincts," 305.
10. Queerness may be too strong. In philosophy of science, it is well known that there is a distinction between *seeing something* and *seeing something as*. It is common for young clinical student not to recognize or see a patient's presentation as an example of a learnt concept. He may see a manic patient's presentation as manic. For the standard discussion, see N. R. Hanson, *Patterns of Discovery: An Inquiry into the Conceptual Foundations of Science*, Cambridge: Cambridge University Press, 1958 or, for a epistemological account, R. M. Chisholm, *Perceiving: A Philosophical Study*. Ithaca, NY: Cornell University Press, 1957.
11. R. J. Bocock, "Freud and the Centrality of Instincts in Psychoanalytic Sociology," *British Journal of Sociology*, vol. 28, no. 4, 1977, 474–75.
12. Jacques Lacan, *Écrits: A Selection* (London: Tavistock Publications, 1977), 102.
13. Jacques Lacan, *The Seminar. Book II. The Ego in Freud's Theory and in the Technique of Psychoanalysis*, trans. Sylvana Tomaselli (Cambridge: Cambridge University Press, 1988), 326.
14. Jacques Lacan, *Écrits: A Selection* (London: Tavistock Publications, 1977), 844.
15. Jacques Lacan, *Le Séminaire. Livre XVII. L'envers de la psychanalyse, 1969–70*, ed. Jacques-Alain Miller (Paris: Seuil, 1991), 51.
16. André Green, *The Work of the Negative*, trans. Andrew Weller (London: Free Association Books, 1999), 205–21.
17. André Green, "Repetition Compulsion and the Pleasure Principle," http://internationalpsychoanalysis.net/wp-content/uploads/2007/10/greenberlin.pdf, 18–19, accessed 23 Apr. 2017.
18. Michael M'Uzan, *Death and Identity: Being and the Psycho-Sexual Drama* (London: Karnac Books, 2013), 176.
19. Michael M'Uzan, *Death and Identity*, xiv.
20. Michael M'Uzan, *Death and Identity*, 4–5.
21. Michael M'Uzan, *Death and Identity*, 15.
22. Michael M'Uzan, *Death and Identity*, 69.
23. Jean Laplanche, "The So-Called 'Death Drive': A Sexual Drive," *British Journal of Psychotherapy*, vol. 20, no. 4, 2004, 455–56.
24. Richard Wollheim, *Sigmund Freud* (Cambridge: Cambridge University Press, 1971), 201.
25. One reason that some analysts may not be the least troubled by these accusation is that they are not realists about the references of their formulations. If clinicians are doing what they are doing as clinicians, a conception having a cash value—it assists them in case formulation—may suffice. They might well say, if the patient I am treating is not a Freudian system, I shall have to shift to some other framework to understand or tool kit to treat him. And if one is

thinking the conception is a tool, complaints about its cogency may seem bizarre. If faced with a nail, a saw isn't of much use, but it seems odd to complain about the cogency of a saw or raise objections to saws, perhaps while generally lavishing praise on lathes.

26. Allan Compton, "The Current Status of the Psychoanalytic Theory of Instinctual Drives," 382.

27. This is the kind of lax thinking that can be infuriating. Aggression can have external stimuli as it can have a sexual motive, for example, an appetizing person, as anybody with an experience of sexual arousal can testify after a moment's thought.

28. Allan Compton, "The Current Status of the Psychoanalytic Theory of Instinctual Drives," 382–83.

29. See Andre Green, "Repetition Compulsion and the Pleasure Principle," http://internationalpsychoanalysis.net/wp-content/uploads/2007/10/greenberlin.pdf, 4–5, accessed 21 May 2017.

30. Brian Johnson, "Just What Lies 'Beyond the Pleasure Principle'?" *Neuro-Psychoanalysis*, vol. 10, no. 2, 2008, 202–210.

31. Brian Johnson, "Just What Lies 'Beyond the Pleasure Principle'?" 210.

32. Nicole F. Kirman, "The Repetition Compulsion Revisited," *Issues in Psychoanalytic Psychology*, vol. 18, no. 1, 1996, 42 and 47.

33. Cordelia Schmidt-Hellerau, "Libido and Lethe: Fundamentals of a Formalized Conception of Metapsychology," *International Journal of Psycho-Analysis*, vol. 78, 1997, 685.

34. Cordelia Schmidt-Hellerau, "Libido and Lethe," 691 and 695.

35. Norman Lear, *Freud* (New York: Routledge, 2006), 161.

36. Jean Piaget, *The Origin of Intelligence*, trans. M. Cook (New York: International University Press, 1952), 34.

37. Daniel Juda, "Exorcising Freud's 'Daemonic' Compulsion to Repeat: Repetition Compulsion a Part of the Adaptational/Maturational Process," *Journal of the American Academy of Psychoanalysis*, vol. 11, no. 3, 1983, 363 and 365.

38. Joseph Lichtenberg, *Psychoanalysis and Infant Research* (Hillsdale, NJ: The Analytic Press, 1983), 153 and 159.

39. Joseph Lichtenberg, *Psychoanalysis and Infant Research*, 209.

40. A. H. Modell, *Other Times, Other Realities: Toward a Theory of Psychoanalytic Treatment* (Cambridge: Harvard University Press, 1996), 63.

41. Hans-Jurgen Wirth, "Freud, Death, and Creativity," *Psychoanalytic Review*, 90(4), 2003, 594–95.

42. Fred Busch, "The Compulsion to Repeat in Action: A Developmental Perspective," *International Journal of Psycho-Analysis*, vol. 70, 1989, 540.

43. Fred Busch, "The Compulsion to Repeat in Action," 543.

44. Fred Busch, "The Compulsion to Repeat in Action," 543.

45. Robert B. Shapiro, "Separation-Individuation and the Compulsion to Repeat," *Contemporary Psychoanalysis*, vol. 21, no. 2, 1985, 302 and 307.

46. Arnold Wilson and Carol Malatesta, "Affect and the Compulsion to Repeat: Freud's Repetition Compulsion Revisited," *Psychoanalysis and Contemporary Thought*, vol. 12, no. 2, 1989, 266–72.

47. Paul Libby Russell, "The Uses of Repetition," *Smith College Studies in Social Work*, vol. 76, nos. 1 & 2, 2006, 52.

48. Roderick J. Ørner and Peter Stolz, "Making Sense of Repetition Phenomena by Integrating Psychotraumatology and Psychodynamic Psychotherapy," *Journal of Traumatic Stress*, vol. 15, no. 6, 2002, 465–471.

49. This last difficulty, of course, is applicable as well to his early theory of drives.

Conclusion

Dr. Holowchak and I have presented a reading of Freud's thinking on repetition and its relation to the death drive. Both of us believe the reading is an attractive and defensible one. We do have disagreements that periodically surface in the text. Anybody familiar with human minds may well be astonished to find so few disagreements in so many pages. Some disagreements did not seem worth highlighting in the text; others did. And I admire Dr. Holowchak's having managed to do the bulk of the writing without creating more sources of disagreement than emerged.

People disagree for many different reasons. In this book, I would say Dr. Holowchak represents the philosopher's point of view. I am the clinician and, unlike Dr. Holowchak, I am a Freudian. It is that perspective that colors my clinical work. I also think it is a perspective from which the clinician will only be dragged crying and screaming. It is this divide between the perspective of the philosopher and the clinician that both of us hopes has led to creative inactions but also accounts for difficulties reaching agreement on many central matters. For example, an observation of Betty Joseph[1] regarding the repetition and death instinct resonates with me. "Freud postulated that the repetition compulsion was a manifestation of the death instinct at work describing the death instinct as tending towards the reinstatement of the previous state of existence, in the final issue to an inorganic state," and noted a class of patients who "feel most free from anxiety when they can become near to inorganic—that is, free of emotions, and this is, in part, what they aim to aid. The patients in question are those whose lives have repetitive, apparently passive, unhappy experiences. For example, patients who again and again attract love without loving back and who fear dependency on a lover for fear of being let down." Joseph's paper brings Freud's thinking into clinical relief in a way that no philosophical work can. The clinical example helps explain why clinicians may cling to their practices even when their philosophical justification seems feeble. They continue to do their work in the way they learned to do in it (John Forrester helps to explain why).[2] Doing the work creates conviction that is hard for mere argument to overturn. In any event, in a nonscholarly way, I wish to identify some central areas of contention between Dr. Holowchak and me.

Like many clinicians I do not view all of Freud's speculations on large topics to my taste. If he had never written *Moses and Monotheism*, *Totem and Taboo*, and *Civilization and its Discontents*, I would feel psychoanalysis might well in better repute than the decaying theory it is often scolded for being today in a wide range of analytic philosophers' writings, including, but not limited, to Crews, Glymour, Kitcher, and Laudan. When Freud turns anthropologist, even worse, turns biologist, or master of *Geisteswissenschaft*, I advise anybody with a taste for accurate anthropology, biology, or human sciences to stop up their ears. In his clinical work and papers, there emerges an account of the human mind and how to treat what Freud called neurotic suffering that I believe shows Freud at his best. I prefer my psychoanalysis as a sui generis science. Freud's pre-psychoanalytic work did have an impact on his thinking. It is visible for anybody to see in his *Scientific Project*, but there may well be a reason the *Project* never amounted to anything. It was not psychoanalytic. Psychoanalysis offers a path to understanding a patient, not the patient's neurons. Hence philosophers, for example Kitcher, wishing to cast Freud as a biological scientist, rather than psychoanalyst, do so at their peril.[3]

The goal of analysis is an augmentation of a patient's ability to love and work. As it happens, a deep understanding of why we do what we do and the role, especially when we are stuck, of our secret pasts that accumulate in our "unconscious," which incidentally is not a place in the brain like the amygdala is, helps most human beings get unstuck. Getting unstuck tends to make it easier to love and work. I would add it even opens up the possibility of a spiritual life in many people. Nor is psychoanalysis the sole means of psychological help. Ever since Jerome Frank,[4] and more recently Bruce Wampold,[5] researchers have recognized the rough therapeutic equivalence of different schools of treatment, the so-called Dodo Effect. Psychoanalysis unlike many therapies put an emphasis on self-understanding that biological approaches based on medications do not. By the nature of the case, psychoanalytic understanding is not a biological understanding. Even if, like Prozac, psychoanalysis changes serotonin levels in a patient, psychoanalytic patients do not talk about the reason for their change in those terms. Many fans of biological psychiatry do. Everybody knows that being in a rut, being in the grasp of compulsive, repetitive behavior, occurs. Everybody also knows that getting out of these ruts, indeed with psychoanalytic help or a different treatment, is possible. If so, that much of psychoanalysis is compatible with whatever the last word in biology, chemistry, or physics turns out to be; every bit as compatible as biological treatments that tend to concoct unsubstantiated biological stories instead of psychoanalytic stories.

The least clinically useful of Freud's models, as I think becomes clear in this book, is the economic theory, a model under the influence of potted biological thinking. In the economic model, hydraulics are central. Energy sloshes around in the psychical apparatus. Malign distributions of energy make a patient sick. I as a clinician have never found this way of conceptualizing clinical work useful, except as metaphor. For example, most people have mountain ranges in their minds. There are people, animals, feelings, places, smells, tastes, sights, and all manner of mental representation that loom as mountains, oceans, or vast deserts in a human being's inner world. It can be sometimes useful to speak of these saliencies as, for example, having a high level of cathexis or as being hypercathected. It is sometimes, especially when something that was once a regular preoccupation of a patient ceases to preoccupy him, useful to speak of these saliencies as being decathected. But I don't know that I have ever met an analyst or psychodynamic therapist who believed, aside from the crazy Reich and his followers, an orgone awaiting measurement existed. So I would be very happy to minimize tracing Freud through his biology, though I must admit the passages are there, as Dr. Holowchak reminds me, even if I prefer to dismiss them as unfortunate. Bishop Berkeley had tar water; Freud his peculiar biology.

In fact, my Freud *is* messy. He wrote occasion pieces. He was not Karl Barth, who worked out a massive systematic theory with rigor. Like any good thinker, Freud wanted to achieve consistency in his thought, but when you write as Freud did it is not easy to come by. Clinical work keeps shoving surprises in a clinican's face. Freud also had a tendency to hoard. By the time he joined the structural model to the signal theory of anxiety in 1926, along with a dual theory of drives, his new model, the Structural Theory, contradicted the theoretical models Freud had already built—the psychodynamic, the economic and the topographic—when he wrote his two great works the *Interpretation of Dreams* and *Three Essays on Sexuality*. He had come to recognize in the 1920s that the mind is not organized as he imagined it to be in the first decade of the twentieth century. Although he edited his great works repeatedly during his life he did not rewrite them. My guess is that he did not rewrite for one reason. He would have had to do a total redux, as the accounts of mental functioning in the two great works are based on an account of mind that is inconsistent with his final theory, the structural theory. There is no censor in the structural theory as there is in the two great works. Instead, dreams are compromise formations. There is no superego in these early great writings nor is there an easy place for defense analysis. Instead, analysis is an effort to uncover the unconscious. The structural theory coincided with the ascendency of defense analysis. In defense analysis, the analyst seeks to reveal an unconscious ego function, the defenses. Over time repeated defense interpretations allow more previously unconscious material to emerge in a patient's associations. The process is laborious and slow. Over time, material from the id does become available to the patient. The goal is *Wo es war, soll ich warden*: Where It was, I shall be. Psychoanalysis has become a prescription for self-knowledge.

The final prescription would include an understanding of why one was stuck and, constantly, given to repeating failed solutions. On the signal theory of anxiety, repetition occurs because hazardous unconscious wishes and impulses are in danger of becoming conscious. The defenses are like an alerted policeman who scares the danger away. Anxiety drops, but of course the intruders return, as does anxiety. The patient is stuck. As it happens, my experience is that a common reason for a human being getting stuck has to do with sexual and aggressive drives. Whether one views these *Triebe* as inborn or not, much of childhood targets the expression of these wishes and impulses. If a boy expresses a desire to see his mum naked or to hurt his father, these may get sanctioned. In some cases, people learn to deny these feelings of sexual interest or aggression so completely that they become invisible. Perhaps a patient will claim that he never had a desire to see his mother naked or that when he did he hated it. He may claim he never desired to hurt Father's massive masculinity. He may say he is unable to shower with other men owing to his being a modest person, rather than notice that seeing penises makes him anxious, an anxiety he may later recognize as driven by a desire to hurt men (his father). This recognition leads to him being able to tolerate male nudity without anxiety, and perhaps some agreement at how much rage and violent wishes his "modesty" had in it. In that sense, Eros and death drive, despite their transformation in contemporary psychoanalysis, has continued. Therapists know how ubiquitous the problems of regulating sexuality and aggression are. They also know how being stuck with one solution leads to repetition.

But this chain of reasons and conjectures about why Freud did not rewrite his two great works to bring them into conformance with the structural theory is but one reason he did not rewrite them. The other reason is something I believe as a clinician and something the analyst Fred Pine noted. The different Freudian models are, whatever their faults, different devices for understanding patients. Pragmatism, which always carries some antirealism with it, refuses to surrender a perspective, if it affords insights more readily than alternatives. *The Theory of Dreams* and the *Three Essays* seem to me to reduce the labor needed to understand dreams and sexuality. Whether they are literally true or cohere with later work is beside the point. Their justification is their ability to understand patients and their thoughts, feelings, and behavior. To some this may sound disreputable. I doubt it is uncommon. In the social sciences, it does happen. One of the most used instruments for measuring psychopathology is *the Minnesota Multiphasic Personality Inventory*. Two forms of it are now common the MMPI-2 and the MMPI-RF. Long after everybody had stopped using the diagnostic categories of the MMPI's original authors, for example scales for Hypochondriasis, Depression, Hysteria, Psychopathic Deviate, Masculinity/Femininity, Paranoia, Psychasthenia, Schizophrenia, Hypomania, and Social Introversion, the inventory continued in use. Empirical research was conducted with it. Scoring patterns for newer DSM diagnoses were mapped. Clinicians and researchers can continue to ask good questions with good answers using the MMPI. They could ask, for example, about its predictive validity for identifying persons more likely to have complaints if hired as corrections officers. They need not believe in the original or current diagnostic constructs of the MMPI to answer that question. And so it is, despite the truth of the topographic theory, on Freud's own accounting, being rejected, analysts can still use the theory to interpret dreams, and often do so with results that satisfy themselves and their patients. Philosophers and other outsiders are harder to please. The harshest critics of psychoanalysis are often people no more likely to get on the couch than Galileo's fiercest critics were to use a telescope. If a student of Freud can accept this amount of antirealism, Freud makes a better companion, as the student will stop making demands for consistency.

In spelling out Freud's theories, I often find myself in disagreement with the undue emphasis on the etiology of neuroses. It's a common enough approach to Freud, as it is easy to spot the etiological accounts of disorders. Focus on etiology can also seem to have the advantage of showing psychoanalysis as doctrines open to refutation. Grunbaum made much of this fact when he bashed Freud's account of paranoid schizophrenia.[6] The clinician in me is unimpressed. Etiological accounts of illness are born to die. The history of medicine is littered with mistaken etiologies. The dopamine theory of schizophrenia is one example, but you can page through issues of *The American Journal of Psychiatry* and find a treasure-trove of ill-fated hypotheses about psychiatric disorders. One of the underpinnings of Thomas Szasz's famed argument that mental illness is a myth used the sorry state of psychiatric etiologies. Even in positivist terms the undamaging nature of refuted etiologies is no mystery. Etiologies are at the edge of a theory. They are among the first hypotheses that can be jettisoned without damage to central features of a theory. In physical medicine, a discovery that an alternative etiology produces the disease rather than the received one make few ripples in the world of physical medicine. What would be a sea change would be the bona fide discovery (neither Dr. Holowchak nor I are holding our breath) of a supernatural etiology. Freud's critics exaggerate the importance of Freud's theoretical revisions and how they led to his inaccurate accounts of various disorders' etiologies. Mistaken psychoanalytic etiologies for disorders do not disrupt the core of psychoanalytic theory, only their peripheries.

I propose to be dogmatic and assert that the true drivers of revision to psychoanalytic theory were and continue to be psychoanalytic data obtained during psychoanalyses of patients on the couch. Analysts are often notorious for their indifference to diagnoses. Charles Brenner rejected depression diagnosis, viewing it as a mere symptom.[7] I have heard Edward Nersessian, a supervising analyst at the New York Psychoanalytic Institute and friend of neuro-psychoanalysis, as he once edited *Neuro-Psychoanalysis: An Interdisciplinary Journal*, express his utter disdain for the Diagnostic Statistical Manual of the American Psychiatric Association (DSM).[8] For the most part, psychoanalysts are likelier to be concerned about topics like defense. For example, Otto Kernberg[9] has used an axial system. On the x-axis, a patient's introversion and extroversion are rated. Along the y-axis, the analyst rates the defensive organization of a patient as being psychotic, borderline, or neurotic. For one inclined to, one could locate DSM diagnoses using these axes. Most Freudians do not. The Kernberg system does carry clinical implications and a means for marking progress, for example the reliance on more "mature" defense and less repetitiveness in the employment of defenses. I doubt changes in psychoanalytic theory occur because a patient does or does not fit well into Kernberg's schemata. What does drive change is listening, deep listening, to what patients are saying, and then seeking means to make sense of it. To rely on personal experience, suspect oracle though it be, I noticed that as I learned more about psychoanalysis, having different models available to me enabled to me to understand what I once did not. I became far more attentive to projections in therapy hours after I studied Intensive Short-Term Psychodynamic Therapy with Jon Frederickson.[10] Before listening to Frederickson, I tended not to notice that when a patient was telling me in the early stages of therapy, well before I have expressed a view, the patient is then projecting when he says: "You'll think I'm a hot mess. Everybody does. You want me to get better, of course, but what can be done?" This bit of talk is a tissue of projections. I have no view of him being a mess, nor, I suspect, is it true that everybody thinks this. I've said nothing about wanting him to get better. I don't even know what that might mean yet. I might add there is a fair amount of aggressive imposition in these associations. What made me receptive to Frederickson's observations? I claim a lot of hard-earned experience as a therapist. Something clicked. I noticed a whole realm of observation that I had failed to make sense of. In time I may have hit upon the projective defense inherit in this talk of the patient, but pressure, or so I claim, to make these revisions comes from an abundance of clinical experience, not from thinking about the etiologies of the patients I see. It is working from cases. The obstacle to doing reconstructions of Freud's theoretical development from this clinical viewpoint is that much of what is driving the revisions is going to be invisible not only to the scholar doing an exegesis of the texts, but to the author of the texts as well. The brute facts that favor it are a piece of common sense. The longer a person works on a topic the more his initial theories of it change. Of course a John Rawls, a philosopher, has a clear public record of evolving thinking and noticing what drove him to make changes in his theory of justice. Nonphilosophers, or philosophers without the acute gifts and narrow focus of a Rawls, are less likely to have accurate accounts of how their views evolved. Then, too, geniuses often have insights that outrun their ability to justify them. This sometimes happens in mathematics. For example, The Church-Turing Thesis that every effectively calculable function is a computable function was never proved by either of them, or anybody else.

Some of the failures of Dr. Holowchak and me to reach agreement arise from deeper philosophical differences. To that end, we are including a paper on realism and perspectivism in the philosophy of science. Dr. Holowchak is more of a scientific realist than I am. I know, for example, the miasmic theory is filled with false hypotheses about what causes disease. The antibacterial theory is correct theory to rely on if I am thinking about what is causing dysentery at Scutari. Nevertheless, I may find it much easier to know how to proceed and what to encourage others to do if I stick with the miasmic theory, especially if I am training people who believe in fresh air but not bacteria. I encourage more light and fresh air and thorough and regular cleaning of the mire, blood, and dirt in the hospital. The better theory is the superior one, but one can imagine why it might have been easier to get people to act on the miasmic theory in the Crimea than Pasteur's theory.

As a therapist I am used to moving between theories. Early in my career I treated sexual dysfunction in a sexuality clinic with behavioral methods. It is a truth of clinical work that many patients do not do what their therapist asks them to do. I then found myself, after reading Helen Kaplan and Paul Wachtel,[11] moving to psychodynamic work with patients refusing behavioral intervention until I could remove their opposition to them. I once failed to help a man refusing to take Viagra, after he had also not done the behavioral treatments either. We then began to discuss his resistance to taking Viagra. After a fair amount of work, he recognized that his fear of taking Viagra (his signal anxiety) led to all manner of defenses against taking it. He eventually realized that his underlying fear was that if he took it and he did not respond to it, he would not be a man. Once he began to address previously what was unconscious about being a man, he was able to take the Viagra. It worked. After a while, he also discovered he did not need the Viagra. I might add that among some of his views, there was his archaic belief that his penis was a weapon that would hurt women and there were a bounty of parental prohibitions on anger.

Many clinicians are eclectic enough to work from a variety of perspectives. Whether or not the interlocking of the theories is consistent is ignored. Sometimes efforts are made to unite theories as did Dollard and Miller's offering of a behavioral account of psychoanalysis,[12] but they seldom won allegiance over time. Clinicians simply do not insist on the systematic rigor that philosophers do. The appendix paper perhaps simplifies understanding the consideration that kept Dr. Holowchak and me from agreeing on all the key issues. I do find these kinds of disagreements beneficial and a source of the pleasure I obtain from doing work with Dr. Holowchak. I do hope readers appreciate what mixing the rigorous philosophical perspective of Dr. Holowchak with my tendency to think clinically from cases contributed to our book.

NOTES

1. B. Joseph, "An Aspect of the Repetition Compulsion," *Psychic Equilibrium and Psychic Change*, eds. M. Feldman and E. B. Spillius (London: Routledge, 1958), 32.
2. J. Forrest, *Thinking in Cases* (Cambridge, UK: Polity, 2016).
3. P. Kitcher, *Freud's Dream: A Complete Interdisciplinary Science of Mind* (Boston, MA: MIT Press, 1995).
4. J. B. Frank and J. D. Frank, *Persuasion and Healing: A Comparative History of Psychotherapy*, 3rd edition (Baltimore: Johns Hopkins University Press, 1993).
5. B. E. Wampold and Z. E. Imel, *The Great Psychotherapy Debate: The Evidence for What Makes Psychotherapy Work*, 2nd edition (New York: Routledge, 2015).
6. Adolf Grunbaum, *The Foundations of Psychoanalysis: A Philosophical Critique* (Berkeley: University of California Press, 1984).
7. C. Brenner, *The Mind in Conflict* (Madison, CT: International Universities Press, 1982).
8. *Diagnostic and Statistical Manual of Mental Disorders*, 5th ed. (Washington, DC: Author, 2007).
9. O. F. Kernberg, *Severe Personality Disorders: Psychotherapeutic Strategies* (New Haven, CT: Yale University Press, 1984).
10. Jon Frederickson, *Psychodynamic Therapy: Learning to Listen from Multiple Perspectives* (New York: Routledge & Frederickson, 1999), and *Co-creating Change: Effective Dynamic Therapy Techniques* (Kansas City, MO: Seven Leaves Press, 2013).
11. H. S. Kaplan, *The New Sex Therapy* (New York: Routledge, 1974); P. L. Wachtel, *Psychoanalysis, Behavioral Therapy and the Relational World* (Washington, D.C.: American Psychological Association, 1997); and P. L. Wachtel, *Relational Theory and Psychoanalysis* (New York: Guilford, 2008).
12. J. Dollard and N. E. Miller, *Personality and Psychotherapy* (New York: McGraw-Hill, 1950).

A Reading of Freud's Epistemology

Realism or Perspectivism?

There are a number of occasions where Freud defended psychoanalysis from criticisms by assuming the role of philosopher of science. At such times, his aim was often to defend psychoanalysis by offering a general sketch of scientific methodology and of the practice of science, learned when working in Brucke's laboratory, and then showing how psychoanalysis is consistent with the methods he learned in his early years as a laboratory scientist. Such passages in Freud are congruent with what is nowadays called to scientific realism. Of course one must be careful not to read too much of today's vocabulary back into Freud. For better or worse, Freud wrote occasion pieces in which he responded to puzzles arising in the context of the psychoanalytic practice and writing of his day. Further because Freud's active working life lasted about forty years during which his thinking was constantly evolving, caution is required when attributing systematic views to him, especially when he was responding to a critic, rather than working out his own views relative to the clinical material he encountered in his work as a psychoanalyst.

Though Freud was no philosopher, he was, however, aware of the difficulties with realism, including of the difficulties with assuming that there can be objective knowledge of the world around us, or in Thomas Nagel's terms, a "view from nowhere" (1989). Freud addressed those difficulties straightforwardly, but not fully, in later works like *Future of an Illusion* and "The Question of a *Weltanschauung*." The problems with realism, he noted, were not just problems for psychoanalysis, given its analysis of the psychical apparatus that biologists and biophysicists used to examine the physical world. Realism's multiple problems were, he recognized, problems with which all scientists had to grapple. And, again, one must keep in mind that in German what counts as a science is broader than what counts in English, as German incudes *Geisteswissenschaft*—a branch of science broad enough to include Law and History.

We shall offer one interpretation of Freud's epistemological views, sketched out mostly in *Future of an Illusion*, which he believed captures his mature view. We ask whether perspectivism, proposed as a compromise or in-between position between realism and relativism, better captures a defensible interpretation of Freud's views than an interpretation based on realism.

We begin with a gloss of scientific realism and scientific relativism, and then turn to scientific perspectivism. Next, we offer one reading of Freud's epistemological views, which make substantive concessions to both objectivism and subjectivism. Overall, we argue that Freud is taken best as a perspectivist.

A caveat is in order. Our reading of Freud's epistemology is a reading of a line of thought that Freud has sketched out in later writings, not spelled out. As a result our reading depends on speculation of what Freud could have said, had he given the matter fuller thought. We cannot offer a definitive critical assessment of passages in Freud's work that establish our reading. Consequently, we aim at categorizing, not criticizing, his embryonic epistemology.

For the purposes of this undertaking, the characterizations we give of scientific realism, scientific relativism, and scientific perspectivism are selective and certainly cannot do justice to the full range of contemporary scholarship.

SCIENTIFIC REALISM

There is no one commonly accepted definition of "scientific realism" to which all scientific realists adhere. It is best to proceed by elaborating on a view that offers a clear depiction of an orthodox version of scientific realism.

Richard Boyd, a philosopher at Cornell, has made numerous contributions to contemporary understandings of scientific realism. He has argued that scientific realism embodies four key theses: what might be dubbed the confirmatory, referential, objectivist, and progressivist theses—hereafter, the CROP theses.

Confirmatory Thesis: Scientific theories are in some measure confirmable,

Referential Thesis: Theoretical terms are referring terms,

Objectivist Thesis: The reality scientific theories describe is largely independent of human thoughts or theoretical commitments, and

Progressivist Thesis: The historical progress of mature science is a matter of closer approximation to the way the world is

The confirmatory thesis commits scientists to a certain methodology of science. Hypotheses generate predictions and predictions are investigated to discover whether they are true or false. True predictions are confirmatory evidence of the truth of the hypothesis that implies them. False predictions roughly disconfirm the hypothesis—"roughly," because not all cases of disconfirmation are cases in which it is reasonable to throw out a hypothesis.

The referential thesis commits scientists to a reality behind the words to which the words refer—a reality to which the words correspond. It is an area of enormous controversy. For example, when Harvey concluded that the heart is a pump that pushes blood through conduits, nobody was prone to think the heart had no reference or a new reference because, prior to Harvey, nobody had come close to establishing the heart was a pump. What people did challenge was the hypothesis that blood was always contained in conduits like veins and arteries. At the time of Harvey, many people observed blood in areas where no veins were apparent. Harvey offered the hypothesis of capillaries, conduits too small to be observed by the naked eye. Malpighi, the Italian microscopist, subsequently observed capillaries (Dampier, 1961, 120). Similar stories exist about many scientific entities. The social sciences have a harder time putting their theoretical entities on display. General intelligence, for example, is inferred on psychometric and other grounds. It is not observed in the way that a capillary, amoeba, distant planet, electrons, or a Higgs-Boson particle is. Freud's id, ego, and superego are functionally defined and the evidence for them is far weaker than entities observed with special equipment or that are used in well-designed experiments.

The objectivist thesis commits scientists to an independently existing reality that is in large part described by theories that are not wish- or commitment-driven. Scientific theories are believed to save the familiar phenomena but also to predict the behavior of theoretic entities. This requirement is rejected by some philosophers—for example Nancy Cartwright (1983) and Ian Hacking (1983). Cartwright and Hacking are entity realists who are skeptical of scientific laws. For them, "laws" are convenient, but rarely accurate, and are routinely revised. Laws literally are false. Nevertheless, entities, like atoms, are real. The laws for atoms that the Greeks, Romans, and other early scientists used to describe them are in history's dustbin, but scientists and engineers today use "atom" as a matter of routine, whatever the inscrutable truth about them may be. Objectivists dislike this account, preferring verisimilitude that increases over time, which fits with their acceptance of Boyd's progressivist thesis.

The progressivist thesis commits scientists to the view that science is a cumulative body of data. Scientific hypotheses allow for an ever-better or ever-correct depiction of reality. The mistaken models and hypotheses of past scientists are jettisoned or revised in favor of a model with greater verisimilitude. Supplantation of Aristotelian physics with Galilean/Newtonian physics occurs only because the latter is a closer approximation to the real physical state of affairs. The same is true of supplantation of Galilean/Newtonian physics with that of Einstein's General Theory of Relativity. There is no possibility of a return to such untenable views. Linked to this idea is the requirement that new theories can account for the same range of phenomena but can also account for new phenomena that have accumulated and that often seem to have no solution on the old theory. Ordinary accounts of Freud include his abandonment of the seduction hypothesis for the wish-fulfillment hypothesis. If one accepts, as Eissler (2001) argues we should, Freud's account, Freud renounced the seduction theory, because molestation was not a sine qua non of neurosis. Psychodynamic factors, not traumata of molestation, best fit with the evidence at Freud's disposal regarding the causation of neuroses. His numerous, repeated, subsequent revisions, including his move to a structural theory, can be viewed, if one has a realistic picture of Freud's work, as evidence driven, just as his rejection of the seduction hypotheis was. Accordingly, these revisions are examples of theoretical progression.

Overall Boyd's four theses are a realist description of what scientists do. Science does not merely save the observable phenomena. Science establishes what exists and how the world is put together. The things and processes science discovered are real and are causally responsible for what we observe, whether it be lasers or differences in doing math problems. Moreover, realist science holds that human beings have access to and can (often) interact with what they thought existed before they got going on science. But, from a realist perspective, *a realm of theoretical processes and entities are the actual building blocks of the world human beings experience.* Of course, the real-world objects of science are often substantially different from those objects of everyday perception. Tables are not much like the atoms that compose them. Of course scientists also study easy-to-spot objects like cacti, octopodes, and even manufactured items like TV sets, and solar panels, as well as realms invisible to the naked eye—realms of dreams, black holes, subconscious phenomena, muons and photons, dark matter, and oceanic trenches. Anybody skeptical about the reality of the theoretical, often invisible entities of sciences, especially sciences like chemistry and physics, face an obvious challenge

Hilary Putnam is blunt about it. His argument from miracles captures the four Boydian theses:

> And a natural account of the way in which scientific theories succeed each other—say, the way in which Einstein's Relativity succeeded Newton's Universal Gravitation—is that a partially correct, partially incorrect account of a

> theoretical object—say, the gravitational field, or the metric structure of space-time, or both—is replaced by a *better* account of the same object or objects. But if these objects do not really exist at all, then it is a *miracle* that a theory which speaks of gravitational action at a distance successfully predicts phenomena; it is a miracle that a theory which speaks of curved space-time successfully predicts phenomena; and the fact that the laws of the former theory are derivable, 'in the limit,' from the laws of the latter theory has no methodological significance. (1984)

Most scientific realists accept the referential thesis. Truth is correspondence of terms and statements with things and states of affairs in the world. By contrast, for typical non-realist accounts of science, truth is coherence. It is a matter of logical consistency of statements in an ever-growing network of accepted truths where the larger the network, the greater the likelihood that the system saves the phenomena and allows for a coherent ordering of past, present, and future experience. A typical instance of this kind of thinking is defended with ingenuity by Bas Van Fraasen (1980) in his *Scientific Image.* Van Fraasen rejected the idea that full scientific descriptions require commitments to unobserved entities. It is enough, for him, if a theory is "empirically adequate," meaning that its laws predict and retrodict what is actually observed.

In any event, for the realist Boyd, scientific terms both map on to real-world objects and are regulated by complex causal interactions with them. For scientific terms like "black hole," "electron," and "unconscious," he writes, "a (type) term *t* refers to some entity *e* just in case complex causal interactions between features of the world and human social practices bring it about that what is said of *t* is, generally speaking and over time, reliably regulated by the real properties of *e*." In short, through investigation, human beings come to know something about real-world objects, because they act on and are acted on by those real-world objects, and their language adjusts to fit the way things are. What regulates the "real features of the world" is the ideal truth of the background theories or theoretical presuppositions that we have of the world (1984).

Overall, for Boyd, there is causal interaction between the real world—the object of scientific investigation—and the scientists that interact with it and write about it. Scientists use specific terms and descriptions to designate and depict the objects they investigate and to explain their behavior. In such a manner, the causal properties of real-world objects function as mechanisms to correct scientific theories and put them on the path toward a better depiction of the way things really are. For instance, if Freud's systemic unconscious exists, then continued study and causal interaction with it will give us more information about it that will enable us to refine existing theories or perhaps develop new theories about it. In short, for Boyd, science is a social practice that allows for a meaningful, causal interaction with the real world.

In such a manner, science allows us in some measure to know the objects with which human beings interact.

There are many criticisms of scientific realism. Let us begin with one pressing objection: the theory-ladenness of scientific statements and concepts. Scientific statements and concepts, the objection states, are theory-dependent, not theory-independent, as many realists claim. Scientific concepts and statements have meaning only within the context of a particular theoretical framework that gives them their meaning—there is no such thing as a theory-independent term or statement. Meaning, then, cannot be determined by the fit of terms and statements to the real world independently of a theoretical framework.

The full weight of the objection comes out in an argument given by Hilary Putman, in a work where he disavows his early views on realism (1988). For Putnam, each person is born with a psychic apparatus that functions by categorizing what it intakes—the raw data of experience. That psychic faculty, what he calls a "commonsense scheme," is roughly the same for each person and allows for certain ways of conceptualizing experiences and disallows other ways—especially when it comes to certain key conceptions like "object" and "existence."

Putnam gets his argument off the ground by an analogy. He asks readers to consider a cookie cutter and dough. The dough represents the material from which perception arises; the cookie cutter represents the way in which human beings form the material, which presumably is widely shared. Encounters with Bowser lead English speakers to announce they are, say, seeing a dog. "But," Putnam adds, "this 'cookie cutter' metaphor founders on the question, 'What are the parts of the dough?'" That question does not admit of only one definitive answer.

To illustrate, Putnam had readers consider a plane and its points. Do planes comprise points (as more fundamental parts of a whole) or should points merely be considered to be limits of planes (in which case the planes are fundamental)? The answer to that question, Putnam thinks, depends on whether one conceives of points as entities or limits—how one, as it were, cuts the dough (1988). There is no "right" answer to the question that further experience will resolve. Reality neither does nor could dictate an answer—a point also reasserted by Van Fraasen in 2010.

SCIENTIFIC RELATIVISM

Paradigm-relativism, introduced to philosophy of science by historian of science Thomas Kuhn (1996), asserts that scientists are not in the business of searching for truths about an independently existing world. For paradigm-relativists, scientific practice is relativistic. It is a matter of solving problems that occur within a given scientific community during the practice of normal science.

Such problems are soluble by employing only those concepts of a community in a manner that is consistent with other acceptable claims within that community. Science, thus, relies on paradigms (Kuhn, 1996, 23) (i.e., patterns or exemplars)—ways of seeing the world that both address and provide the framework for solving existing problems facing a scientific community and anticipate other problems in a community. In addition paradigms are specimens of a scientific community's accepted way of doing science. In particular, paradigms generate, though they are not defined by, their own methodologies and rules. Though consistency within a paradigm is important, it is not essential. New paradigms arise out of antecedent paradigms in answer to problems that prior paradigms could not handle. Though one paradigm arises out of another, the concepts of each paradigm are said to be incommensurable—each has its own language and neither paradigm is reducible to or translatable in terms of the language of the other paradigm. So, as Ellenberger (1981) in his *Discovery of the Unconscious* has said, with psychoanalysis, Freud established a new way of doing psychodynamic psychiatry. Sulloway (1992) expanded the argument by contending that Freud built the psychoanalytic way of doing business by biologizing the antecedent psychodynamic understanding of mind that can traced back at least as far as Mesmer. That makes scientific communication between different scientific communities—such as earth-centered Ptolemaists and sun-centered Copernicans or even Psychoanalysts and Behaviorists—strictly speaking impossible. Behaviorism's methods and concepts trace back to Pavlov's conditioning experiments. Freud's methods and concepts do not. If Kuhn is right and Ellenberger and Sulloway have their history right, translators of psychoanalysis into behaviorism are destined always to get it wrong, though they may well succeed in fooling themselves. There is no bona fide translation of id and superego conflict into behaviorist language, any more than there is a psychoanalytic translation of operant conditioning into psychoanalytic language.

For paradigm-relativists, the choice between models of reality is not solely based on rational factors, such as fit with observable reality or explanatory power. Since scientists must select theories based on non-decisive evidence, it cannot be progressive in the way Boyd thinks. Science, for Kuhnians, is an ineluctably social, not a formal, activity that answers to the needs of people, not to the dictates of Boydian rationality.

Overall, for Kuhn, science is not progressive in the realist sense. Instead, science is problem-solving. As the problems of one time or culture are not the same as the problems of another, so too do the problems of science differ within different scientific communities over time. Problems, then, generate scientific practice, which defies description through any sort of immutable logical analysis to one correct, evidence-dictated theory of everything. In psychoanalysis, for example, the disputes between Kleinians and ego psychologists have this character. Kleinians tend to view themselves as the continuers of Freud's id psychology.So they think Ego psychology is a departure from the mainline of psychoanalysis. Ego psychology led to Freud's structural theory that Freud fully elaborated in 1926 with his discovery of-what he called signal anxiety, whereas Kleinian theory continued to stress drives. Signal anxiety, of course, once recognized, makes defense work central in the therapeutic work of the structural psychoanalyst because, according to the structural theory, anxiety leads to defenses that prevent unconscious wishes and impulses from becoming conscious. In a sense, on the structural theory, patients regulate their anxiety with defenses that prevent them from dealing with their underlying cause, the wishes and impulses that trigger the anxiety. No obvious evidence from within psychoanalysis has succeeded in forcing one of these theories of psychoanalytic phenomena over the other. This was for many years easiest to discern in the psychoanalytic politics in England, where candidates had to choose a training analyst from the ego psychologists, Kleinians, or Independents.

How, though, do problems move science on a Kuhnian description? Within a scientific community, there are periods of normal science in which a paradigm, like Ptolemaic geocentrism, becomes established and remains unchallenged by rival paradigms. Problems or anomalies emerge in time. Yet no single anomaly is sufficient to pose a significant threat to a paradigm. When enough anomalies surface to challenge a dominant paradigm, a scientific revolution may ensue. Kuhn elaborates, "Scientific revolutions are . . . those non-cumulative developmental episodes in which an older paradigm is replaced in whole or in part by an incompatible new one" (1996, 91). A new paradigm, having its own language and rules and being incommensurable with the old one, replaces the old one, "whole or in part," in an effort to solve the problems the old paradigm could not solve. Scientists now *see* and *live in* a different world. Problem-solving ability, however, is not the same as a paradigm's truth or falsity—something entirely outside of the aims of science for Kuhn. Thus, there is nothing in principle disallowing an abandoned paradigm from being adopted later, as a paradigm justifies itself exclusively by its ability to settle current problems, but that is something Kuhn disallows in a later version of his book (1996, 206).

Thus, for Kuhn and other like-minded historians, the error of logical approaches comes precisely in their refusal to examine closely the practice of science in their "discovery" of the logic of science. There is for Kuhn no set-for-all-time logic of science, as this logic is itself endemic to a particular paradigm and can change with a paradigm shift.

There is merit in Kuhn's insistence that philosophical accounts of science square with the practice of science. He is also right in stressing that much of scientific practice has an irrational component.

Still, for many, what seems most troubling in Kuhn is that he maintains science is not in the business of seeking truth—not even in some limited capacity. One wants to say, for instance, that adoption of Galileo's law of falling bodies, $d \approx t^2$, is not merely a matter of a paradigm shift from Aristotelian science, which claims bodies fall in proportion to their weight in some medium, and accepted impetus, impetus being a concept that physics since at least Newton's day has banished. Aristotle's view is just wrong even if it was considered correct in Aristotle's day. Moreover, Kuhn states that different paradigms are not only inconsistent, but are "often actually incommensurable" (1996, 102). That is vague and untrue on realist accounts. That the Copernican world view is incommensurable with Ptolemy's world view is false. First, both were grounded by Aristotle's physics. Second, even if at the time of the emergence of Copernican astronomy, the theories made the same line-of-sight observations, over time, we now know that that planets are in never in actual retrograde motion. There are straightforward reasons for saying Ptolemy was wrong. If Kuhn means that the complete system of propositions of, say, the General Theory of Relativity is a different system and, thus, the two systems are incommensurable, that is certainly is not to say that those persons in different paradigms see different things. They see the same things, but interpret what they see (seeing as) in a different manner.[1] Of course nonrealists may complain that these objections to Kuhn are question begging. It is well to remember that when a theory implies something false, Quine (Quine and Ullian, 1978) has long argued, then how one decides what to give up in one's web of belief is typically decided by considerations that are normative. The desire for conservative, modest, simple, general, and refutable, rather than ascertainably true, theories has much to do with how to handle wayward observations. Whether to abandon a theory, revise it, or dismiss a wayward observation is by what qualities scientists desire a theory to have (viz., conservative, modest, simple general, refutable theories) as truth. When a chemistry class fails to get a hoped-for result on an experiment, neither the class nor its professor thinks the chemical laws have been confounded. Magic that baffles people does not get them to disavow their rudimentary physics. The anomalous observations that led to the jettisoning of ether and ether winds by a new generation of scientists did not dictate the rejection of ether. Competent scientists persisted but died off. While Holowchak believes psychoanalysis is marginal science, Lavin, a friend of psychoanalysis, is concerned that it will die off for social, rather than scientific, reasons. He fears that no matter how cogent a piece of psychoanalytic research may be, nobody will care because fewer and fewer scientists are reading psychoanalytic papers anymore.

In addition to the line of reasoning just described, there have been a variety of sophisticated attempts to overcome the difficulties Kuhn faced from realists, while staying true to his paradigm relativism. Imre Lakatos's work on "research programmes" is one such approach (1970). So too is Larry Laudan's work (1984).[2] Both reject Kuhn's notion of incommensurability, and thus, both reject the notion that paradigms or their equivalents are replaced completely.

Applying Boyd's CROP theses to scientific relativism, we have a rejection of each of the claims that the realist puts forth: theories are not confirmable, theoretical terms are not referring, what theories describe is not independent of human thoughts or theoretical commitments, and modern-day science is not progressive in the realist sense.

SCIENTIFIC PERSPECTIVISM

Perspectivism is a view, generally attributed to Nietzsche, that asserts there is no privileged or God's-eye perspective from which one can gain objective information of reality per se. "There is *only* a perspectival seeing, *only* a perspectival knowing," writes Nietzsche, "and *the more* affects we allow to speak about the matter, *the more* eyes, different eyes, we know how to bring to bear on one and the same matter, that much more complete with our 'concept' of this matter, our 'objectivity' be" (1988, III:12).

Perspectivism attempts reconciliation between realism and relativism by making key concessions to both. It asserts that the information persons glean through their interactions with objects is always information from some particular perspective. Given that, there is no God's-eye or totality-of-all-perspectives view of an object or knowledge. Truth is what humans arrive at when they bring together different perspectives and sort out the differences between them. It makes no sense to speak of truth, independently of any perspective. Nonetheless there is nothing that a priori rules out that the position at which a person arrives when all perspectives are sorted out is not the truth or some approximation of it. About truth, perspectivism is agnostic.

Philosopher Ron Giere has sketched out a philosophy-of-science view of perspectivism to address and propose a solution to the realism/relativism debate. In keeping with scientific realism, Giere proposes, as did Epicurus, that people must take their perceptions of things at face value. That, however, is not to say their perceptions are veridical, but merely that skepticism is no viable option. With perceptions taken at face value, people can then use reasoned discussion to make some sense of them. In keeping with historicism, Giere proposes that scientific claims cannot be divorced from their particular historical and cultural contexts. There is no truth that stands outside of time (13–15).

Acknowledging what Putnam suggests—there are unlimited numbers of theoretical ways of making sense of our experiences and that realism offers no help in deciding between them (88–91)—Giere states that people can do no other than be guided by current perceptions. In short, because the fundamental observations upon which scientific theories rely are observations from some perspective, so too are scientific theories.

Giere takes the perception of color as an example of what he has in mind. Color neither exists in objects, nor does it exist in the minds of human beings. Instead, color is something human beings (and presumably other similarly functioning percipients) see because of their visual system and because of the way the world is (i.e., the nature of light and certain other properties of objects). "Colors are the product of an *interaction* between aspects of the environment and the evolved human visual system." He asks us to consider two persons, a dichromat and a trichromat, looking at a carpet. It is clear that the trichromat will see more colors, but it makes little sense to suppose that the trichromat is really seeing the carpet as it really is—or even closer to the way it really is. Thus, it makes no sense to say that colors exist wholly in the minds of percipients or that colors exist independently of percipients. Colors are due to the interaction between "the material world and human observers." What is true of colors is true of all perceptions. All scientific interaction with the world, from direct observation to observations or measurements with instruments—microscopes or telescopes, subatomic particle detectors, blood-pressure monitors, the analytic couch—are likewise (chaps. 2 and 3).

There are two dimensions that apply to perception and to instruments in the service of perception. The first is that the systems are responsive only to particular kinds of input—human perception to the data suited to sensations; instruments to the data of which they are in service. The second is that all systems make some contribution to the outcome. Thus, there is no way to transcend human perspective in interacting with objects. Other organisms perceive objects differently. Finally, all perspectives are partial. There is no such thing as a complete perspective. That, however, does not imply that each person sees and constructs his own world—his own reality. Each person experiences the world, but is experientially limited by his own perceptions.

For scientific perspectivists, there are, of course, propositions about the world that are embedded in theories, but theories are not generalizations that might be true or false. Theories merely constrain human-constructed models of the world and how its parts work. Truth, then, is a matter of a model's fit with an ensemble of phenomena as experienced from a variety of perspectives.

There are, however, other ways of cashing out scientific perspectivism that are not so relativist-leaning. Let us turn to Freud.

FREUDIAN EPISTEMOLOGY

Though not an epistemologist, Freud tackles a critique of three philosophical positions—nihilism, anarchism, and Marxism—in "The Question of a *Weltanschauung*." Only the first two are relevant to this undertaking.

Intellectual nihilists, drawing incorrectly from relativity theory, try to show that science itself is truth-empty. Freud writes:

> They start out from science [i.e., relativity theory] . . . but they contrive to force it into self-abrogation, into suicide; they set it the task of getting itself out of the way by refuting its own claims. One often has an impression in this connection that this nihilism is only a temporary attitude which is to be retained until this task has been performed. Once science has been disposed of, the space vacated may be filled by some kind of mysticism or . . . by the old religious *Weltanschauung*.

There is no truth—no knowledge of the external world—for nihilists. Scientific truth is the result of human needs and wants, expressed under changing external conditions. Thus, they are illusions. The criterion of truth—correspondence with the external world—is absent. Consequently, all opinions are a "matter of indifference"; all are "equally true and equally false." In such circumstances, truth and falsity are vain (1933, *S.E.*, XXII: 175–76).

The chief defect of nihilism, Freud notes, is that it is self-refuting. Disavowing truth, scientific depictions of reality, like all assertions about reality, are driven by human needs and wants, which change as external circumstances change. Any one opinion is as good as any other opinion, so far as truth goes, though one opinion may answer human needs better than another. Yet with nihilism being just another opinion about reality, there is no reason to think it is true. At best, it is a metatheory of science.

Freud's critique of anarchism is also cogent. Anarchism may be effectively defended in abstract, but its chief defect is that it is contradicted by human actions. "No doubt," says he concerning anarchism, should we embrace anarchism, "we should come upon situations similar to those derived from the familiar paradox of the Cretan who says that all Cretans are liars." He continues:

> All I can say is that the anarchist theory sounds wonderfully superior so long as it relates to opinions about abstract things: it breaks down with its first step into practical life. Now the actions of men are governed by their opinions, their knowledge; and it is the same scientific spirit that speculates about the structure of atoms or the origin of man and that plans the construction of a bridge capable of bearing a load. If what we believe were really a matter of indifference, if there were one such thing as knowledge distinguished among our opinions by corresponding to reality, we might build bridges just as well out of cardboard as out of stone, we might inject our patients with a decagram of

> morphine instead of a centigram, and might use tear-gas as a narcotic instead of ether. But even the intellectual anarchists would violently repudiate such practical applications of their theory. (1933, *S.E.*, XXII: 176)

In short, human beings, by their actions, show that their underlying beliefs are not anarchistic. Their underlying beliefs show a commitment to a reality that is, in some measure, knowable. Yet is that enough to show Freud is a realist?

The Future of an Illusion, written six years earlier, is where Freud addresses directly the issue of the epistemic merit of science—in particular, psychoanalysis. Here he parries the objection that science, "being bound to the conditions of our own organization," can give humans only "subjective results." He briefly gives five observations to parry subjectivism.

> In the first place, our organization—that is, our mental apparatus—has been developed precisely in the attempt to explore the external world, and it must therefore have realized in its structure some degree of expediency; in the second place, it is itself a constituent part of the world which we set out to investigate and it readily admits of such an investigation; thirdly, the task of science is fully covered if we limit it to showing how the world must appear to us in consequence of the particular character of our organization; fourthly, the ultimate findings of science, precisely because of the way in which they are acquired, are determined not only by our organization but by the things which have affected that organization; finally, the problem of the nature of the world without regard to our percipient mental apparatus is an empty abstraction, devoid of practical interest. (1927, *S.E.*, XXI: 55–6)

The first Darwinian observation is powerful. Evolutionary biology requires an organism's capacity for adaptation to surroundings and a certain amount of plasticity in doing so. Freud hinted that a certain part of the mental apparatus—the ego—is the result of the human organism's adaptation to changing circumstances over time. He claimed that the ego, having been molded over millennia—and Freud's use of the passive-voice construction suggests adaptation to circumstances over time—"must . . . have realized in its structure some degree of expediency." That suggests the ego is the psychical structure of adaptation. Through human interaction with the world, the ego has acquired a structure that allows it to glean some knowledge of the world as it is. If not, it has, at least, some capacity to allow human beings to act with a degree of efficiency in it. Let us call this the *argument from adaptation* or AA.

AA: Mental organization (i.e., the ego) has developed in response to human exploration of the external world, so it has realized some degree of expediency, or adaptation.

AA subsequently became part of ego psychology, as developed by Hartman (1939 and 1959), who believed that the psychical apparatus was an adaptation to what Hartman called "the Average Expectable Environment." A serious psychoanalysis ought to be consistent with the theory of evolution.

The second of Freud's observations addresses the issue of subjectivity from the standpoint of allowing the psychical apparatus to be an object of scientific investigation. It is included merely to ward off those critics who allow investigation of external reality, but disallow investigation of the mind. This argument, which we can call the *subject-qua-object argument* or SOA, is fundamental for Freudian psychoanalysis and can be summed up thus:

> **SOA:** The mental apparatus is a part of the world, and admits of scientific investigation via the psychoanalytic method

The method is crucial, as Freud believed that the chief support of psychoanalytic theory comes from psychoanalytic treatment of psychoanalytic patients. This is a point stressed, for example by Edelson (1984 and 1988) and Lavin (2012).

The third observation is critical for Freudian epistemology. It acknowledges the difficulty of the mind, in effect, transcending itself to study itself or the world around it. Science, however, does not have to show how the world is in itself. It does its job, and does it fully, if it shows how the world "must appear to us," given the "peculiar character of our organization"—a decidedly Kantian slant.[3] That is a key concession too subjectivism—a concession that seems too subjectivist. Let us call this the *argument from subjectivity* or AS.

> **AS:** The human psychical apparatus has a peculiar organization, so it affects the way in which humans see and interpret external objects.

AS seems out of keeping with the argument from adaptation. AA and AS seem best reconciled by painting Freud a perspectivist of the Gierian sort, though this could not have been Freud's view at the time, if only because Giere had not even been born. The basic idea we understand as follows. The world presents itself to human beings in a particular way because human beings have evolved in a particular way. Psychoanalysis will have made a contribution if it explains why the human organism structures the sensorium as it does. In modest cases, the psychoanalyst is seeking to understand the reason why an analysand experiences and responds to the world as he does. There is a template for understanding how a particular patient has emerged from psychical organization and his psychical history; however, the mind has the organization it does because of the adaptations to the environment in which human beings have evolved.

The fourth observation of Freud, which we can call the *argument from interaction* or AI, suggests that the activities of scientists, through the methods of science, allow for an interactive approach to the external world. While the argument from adaptation intimates passive adaptation over time to environmental circumstances, the argument from interaction suggest nonevolutionary adaptation through methodological interaction with the objects of scientific investigation; however, there is a similarity between the neurotic and the scientist. Through the methods he uses to attain a nonevolutionary end, the scientist is not in any straightforward sense seeking to reduce signal anxiety, as a neurotic does, but to pursue research questions in his area of expertise.

> **AI:** External objects affect mental organization, so the objects of science are determined both by human mental organization but also by external objects.

Note, however, that again a concession is made to subjectivism. The findings of science are a product of real-world objects and humans' mental organization. AI works with, not independently of, AA and ASM.

Last, there is the *investigation-of-mind argument* or IMA, which reinforces SOA. Whereas SOA focuses on the mind as part of the world, and thereby, as a legitimate object of investigation, IMA focuses on the epistemic priority of mind as an object of study.

> **IMA:** Humans see and grasp the objects of science through their mental apparatus, so investigation of the external world without investigation of the internal world is rather like a decision not to enquire into how a scientific device or mathematical technique works, but just to trust its outputs.

It is reasonable that if real-world objects are to be subjects of scientific investigation, so too should be the psychic apparatus through which they are studied as well as any other devices or techniques. Psychologists, for example, spend a fair amount of time examining the fitness of particular statistical techniques for different types of data sets. In psychoanalysis, one rationale for a training analysis is to calibrate candidate analysts' psychical apparatus. Without this calibration, one might fear a much higher frequency of "bad" forms of countertransference when a candidate psychoanalyzes his "control cases." Thus, IMA is meant to work with AS. Freud recognizes that the objects scientists investigate may be distorted in varying degrees by the psychical apparatus—in other words by the way in which they present to us given the structure of our psychical apparatus.

There are two unexpected results of this analysis at the end of *Future of an Illusion*. First, what seem prima facie to be five independent observations on behalf of scientific objectivity have turned out to be five interlaced arguments that give us an *incipient*, but graspable, epistemology. Second, Freud has made key concessions to subjectivity that make any sort of defense of realism a defense of realism "reals" that are easy to spot in a person's everyday world, not a defense of scientific realism. But is Freud, even if he would have called it something else, defending perspectivism instead?

FREUD: REALIST OR PERSPECTIVIST?

If Freud is a Boydian scientific realist, then he is committed to the CROP theses. Key among them, for our purposes, are the objectivist and the progressivist theses. The objectivist thesis—that the reality scientific theories describe is largely independent of human thoughts or theoretical commitments—is vague, because "largely independent" is vague. The objectivist thesis, in conjunction with the progressivist thesis, at least commits one to a view of science in which the empirical information gleaned through scientific investigation over time is sufficiently independent of human subjectivity and is correctable over time because of the way the world in fact is. If so, some knowledge of external reality is attainable because the methods of scientists over time can often overcome or compensate for the constraints of humans' mental organization. This rendering, if correct, presupposes a "soft" subjectivism.

There are difficulties. First, soft subjectivism seems too weak and inconsistent with AS and AI. Freud, with AI, tells us nothing about the relative contributions of the psychical apparatus and of external objects to scientific knowledge, so one might be tempted, *ceteris paribus*, to assume a relatively equal contribution by each. Second, why must we think that the influence of external objects on the mental apparatus is truth-generating for Freud? AA requires only some degree of evolutionary adaptation. Overall, it runs beyond the texts to conclude that Freud is a scientific realist.

It is also, we have seen, at odds with the texts we have cited to paint Freud a relativist, given his arguments against nihilism and anarchism. His arguments appear as well targeted against what is nowadays called scientific relativism.

What, however, of perspectivism? Perhaps Freud's views fit well with the perspectivist compromise between realism and relativism? AI, as we have seen, makes concessions to objectivism and subjectivism, realism and relativism, and those concessions in effect drive perspectivism.

One problem is Freud's embrace of scientific progressivism, which seems difficult to square with perspectivism. In *Totem and Taboo*—not, incidentally, a towering contribution to anthropological science—Freud mentions the developmental path of three great systems of progressive thought: the animistic (or mythological), the religious, and the scientific (1913, *S.E.*, XIII: 76–77). Elsewhere he writes with a braggart's swagger of three great blows to human narcissism (1917, *S.E.*, XVI: 284–85; 1917, *S.E.*, XVII: 139–41;

and 1925, *S.E.*, XIX: 221)—the last and most devastating of which is psychoanalysis—which Holowchak has argued demonstrates Freud's commitment to scientific progressivism (2010 and 2011). It is this commitment to progressivism he likely has in mind, when he speaks in *Future of an Illusion* of the god Logos and the "distant future" in which the intellect, not the passions, govern human action (1927, *S.E.*, XXI: 53–54). Freud's acceptance of scientific progress seems, once again, to place him in the realist camp, though Lavin thinks certain forms of nonrealism are compatible with scientific progress. For example, if one is nonrealist about laws because they routinely turn out to be false, one can still hold that science is progressing when new laws cover a wider range of phenomena than the old laws without giving rise, in relation to the supplanted theory, to inaccurate predictions or retrodictions, if only because that is a design constraint on a new theory. The structural theory, for example, might be thought to be at large advantage over Freud's earlier topological theory.

Can Progressivism Be Reconciled with Perspectivism?

Perspectivism of the sort that Giere proposes disallows a robust sense of scientific progress that only scientific realism gives. Freud's epistemological views, however, are not Giere's. Freud does not think that there are an indefinitely large number of ways to describe the world, given different theoretical commitments. He arguably thinks that there is only one correct way to describe the world, though modern psychoanalysts like Fred Pine (1990) reject this idea in relation to clinical practice. In addition, Freud does not take what an analysand says at face value. As Holowchak sees it, Freud was committed to subjective and objective worlds—in other words, that our sensory data are representations of real-world objects—and each world comes prominently into play in his epistemology. As Lavin has it, Freud's position on this matter is clinical. There are things a patient says because his sensorium is what it is and the memorable parts of his history are what they currently are. But that is not all; sometimes, via the use of the psychoanalytic method, an analyst makes inferences about the organization and content of an analysand's psychical apparatus and the history that produced it, as well as further facts about the transference. Freud's epistemology is up to making this distinction without resort to larger scale issues about subjective and objective reality. Instead, the goal is to produce a psychoanalytic account of the phenomena under scrutiny.

Overall, though, we believe Freud's five dependent arguments in chapter 10 of *Future of an Illusion*, if they are taken as a defense of realism, express a commitment to an etiolated form of realism that is not Boydian. Accordingly, Freud's position is inconsistent with Boyd's objectivist thesis, which privileges the objective.

Freud's arguments, then, seem to be taken best as a defense of a realist-friendly version of perspectivism, if only because he makes substantive concessions to realism and relativism. It is realist-friendly inasmuch as it allows for the possibility of genuine knowledge of some sort of the external world, because of Freud's own perceived epistemic gains vis-à-vis the human mind that grasps it. The legitimacy of Freud's epistemic gains concerning the psychic apparatus has been the subject of a large body of critical literature. There is considerable debate about what is salvageable (Holowchak, 2012).

UPSHOT

In this appendix, we have attempted the modest project of fleshing out Freud's inchoate epistemological views in *The Future of an Illusion* and other later works, without critical assessment of them.

Concern for epistemological issues was made possible by adoption of his structural model in 1923—specifically, his embrace of the ego, which enabled him to tackle two difficulties: the problem of consciousness as a differentiator of systems and the problem of censorship in dreams.

First, in his 1915 prestructural paper "The Unconscious," Freud says that consciousness, as the only part of the psyche to which we have direct access, "is in no way suited to serve as a criterion for the differentiation of systems." By that, he means it is too episodic and unstable to be the prominent psychical system that allows for some sense of psychical unity. Unconsciouness, having greater stability, is too Cimmerian and mysterious (1915, *S.E.*, XIV: 192)

Second, in *Interpretation of Dreams*, Freud maintains that censorship in dreams is mostly at the hands of *Pcs.*, (1900, *S.E.*, IV: 567–68 and 617). That entails that one can readily be aware of one's own resistance, but not the content of that resistance. Clinical experience, for Freud, suggested that that is false. In most cases of resistance, patients are both unaware of the content of resistance and resistance itself (1923, *S.E.*, XIX: 8). Consequently, Freud believes that a new topography is needed.

Freud's structural model in *The Ego and the Id* in 1923 was an attempt to solve the problems of differentiation and censorship through positing a different, more versatile and stable, psychical entity—the ego. He writes:

> We have formed the idea that in each individual there is a coherent organization of mental processes; and we call this his *ego*. It is to this ego that consciousness is attached; the ego controls the approaches to motility—that is, to the discharge of excitations into the external world; it is the mental agency which supervises all its own constituent processes, and which goes to sleep at night, though even then it exercises the censorship on dreams. (1923, *S.E.*, XIX: 8)

Later he adds that "ego" is the name of that psychical agency that takes in stimuli for internal processes and orients an organism to the external world—that "single superficial system *Pcpt.-Cs.*, (1923, *S.E.*, XIX: 14). "I propose to take it into account by calling the entity which starts out from the system *Pcpt.* and begins by being *Pcs.* the 'ego', and . . . in calling the other part of the mind, into which this entity extends and which behaves as though it were *Ucs.*, the 'id'" (1923, *S.E.*, XIX: 17).

It seems plain that Freud's metapsychological description of his structural model is ad hoc. He needs a coherent agency, linked neatly to reality, in order to solve the problems of group psychology to which he turns in 1913 in *Totem and Taboo* and on which he focuses thereafter. Moreover and more to the point of this essay, without such an agency, there could be no psychoanalytic examinations of the psychical apparatus and, as Holowchak sees it, of the problem of knowing. One of us has misgivings about this part of our reading. Lavin views the need for a Freudian ego as arising from clinical material and the idea that topological model's partitioning of what is conscious and unconscious is inconsistent with the clinical facts. For example, defenses mechanisms, which are ego-functional, are typically, though not always, unconscious.[4]

Nonetheless, was Freud's ego harmfully ad hoc or was it a needed heuristic, an engine making possible future psychoanalytic discoveries about human behavior and pathology that would someday lead to advances in biology? Freud thought the structural model was needed; new psychoanalytic discoveries would be impeded without such a metapsychological step (1923, *S.E.*, XIX: 8). Some psychoanalysts today, ego psychologists especially, would perhaps agree.

Our reading of the texts leads us to a conventional, normative philosophy of science. We do not regret that we engaged in this dispute to clear ground for further discussion on such issues.

Perhaps because of the dominance of Grünbuam (1985), writing on psychoanalysis has had a tendency to ignore a different approach to the philosophy of science that is now called the Stanford School. Members of the school include or have included Nancy Cartwright, John Dupre, Peter Gallison, Ian Hacking, and Patrick Suppes. One hallmark of the Stanford School is its deep appreciation of the importance of detailed history regarding scientific practices. Gallison, for example, has paid meticulous attention to the practices of working physicists in such works as *How Experiments End* and *Image and Logic*. Cartwright has long paid attention to what physicists do, but has also turned to the actual practices of social scientists to better understand their work and claims, for example in *Hunting Causes* and in a book she coauthored with Jeremie Hardie. Thinking about psychoanalysis had a start on this track in B. A. Farrell's *Standing of Psychoanalysis* (1981). Farrell took the time to look at what one psychoanalyst did with his patients.

It is unfortunate that this Stanford-styled work out of Oxford did not have more impact on psychoanalytic writing. We stand by our reading of Freud's epistemology, but also hope that future work will pay much more attention to what psychodynamic clinicians do in their consulting rooms and in their research (such as is seen in B. Milrod et al., 2007).

NOTES

1. See Donald Davidson's "Argument from Translation" (1973–4) for a good account of why relativism of the Kuhnian sort is false. Scheffler (1982) is also useful on many of the general issues.
2. Laudan (1984) says paradigms comprise methodological principles, axiological aims (i.e., values), and theories and that a paradigm shift occurs if at least one changes.
3. Tauber (2010, 96 and 191), who takes Freud to have studied Kant and who asserts that Freud bought into both Kant's phenomenal and noumenal selves, does not ascribe a Kantian epistemology to Freud. When the structural model is in place, there is no totality or self and nothing comparable to Kant's constituent structure of mind to enable a "cognitive construction of reality." He loosely categorizes Freud as a "phenomenologist gathering 'data.'"
4. Lavin views the need for a Freudian ego as arising from clinical material and the idea that the topological model's partitioning of what is conscious and unconscious is inconsistent with the clinical facts. For example, defense mechanisms, which are an ego function, are typically, though not always, unconscious.

REFERENCES

Boyd, R. (1984). "The Current Status of Scientific Realism." *Scientific Realism.* Jarret Leplin (ed.). Berkeley: University of California Press.

Cartwright, N. (1983). *How the Laws of Physics Lie*. Oxford: Clarendon Press.

Dampier, W. C. (1961). *A History of Science and Its Relation with Philosophy and Religion, 4th Edition, with Postscript*. Cambridge: Cambridge University Press.

Davidson, D. (1973–4). "On the Very Idea of a Conceptual Scheme." *The Proceedings and Addresses of the American Philosophical Association*, 47, 5–20.

Edelson, M. (1984) *Hypothesis and Evidence in Psychoanalysis.* Chicago: University of Chicago Press.

Edelson, M. (1988). *Psychoanalysis: A Theory in Crisis*. Chicago: University of Chicago Press.

Eissler, K. R. (2001). *Freud and the Seduction Theory: A Brief Love Affair*. Madison CT: International Universities Press.

Ellenberger, H. (1981). *The Discovery of the Unconscious: The History and Evolution of Dynamic Psychiatry*. New York: Basic Books.

Farrell, B. (1981). *The Standing of Psychoanalysis*. Oxford: Oxford University Press.

Freud, Sigmund. *The Standard Edition of the Complete Psychological Works of Sigmund Freud*, Vols. I–XXIV, ed. and trans. James Strachey (London: The Hogarth Press, 1976).

Giere, R. (2006). *Scientific Perspectivism.* Chicago: University of Chicago Press.

Hacking, I. (1983). *Representing and Intervening: Introductory Topics in the Philosophy of Natural Science*. Cambridge: Cambridge University Press.

Hartmann, H. (1939). *Ego Psychology and the Problem of Adaptation*. New York: International Universities Press.

Hartmann, H. (1959/1964). *Essays on Ego Psychology*. New York: International Universities Press.

Holowchak, M. A. (2012). "When Freud (Almost) Met Chaplin: The Science behind Freud's 'Especially Simple, Transparent Case." *Perspectives on Science*, Vol. 20, No. 1, 44–74.

Holowchak, M. A. (2011). *Freud and Utopia: From Cosmological Narcissism to the 'Soft Dictatorship' of Reason.* Lanham, MD: Lexington Books, 2011), chap. 1.

Holowchak, M. A. (2010). "Technology and Freudian Discontent: Freud's 'Muffled Meliorism' and the Problem of Human Annihilation." *Sophia*, 49(1), 95–111.

Kuhn, T. (1996). *The Structure of Scientific Revolutions.* Chicago: University of Chicago Press.

Lakatos, I. (1970). "Falsification and the Methodology of Scientific Research Programmes." *Criticism and the Growth of Knowledge*. Imre Lakatos and Alan Musgrave (eds.). New York: Cambridge University Press.

Lavin, M. (2012). "On Behalf of Free Association" and "Reply to Grunbaum" in *Radical Claims, Freudian Psychoanalysis: Point/Counterpoin*t. Ed. M. Andrew Holowchak (pp. 153–166 & 183–186). Lanham, MD: Jason Aronson Press.

Laudan, L. (1984). *Science and Its Values*. Berkeley: University of California Press.

Milrod, B., Leon, A. C., Busch, F., et al. (2007). A Randomized Controlled Clinical Trial of Psychoanalytic Psychotherapy for Panic Disorder. *American Journal of Psychiatry, 164: 265–272.*

Nagel, T. (2002). "What Is It Like to Be a Bat?" *Philosophy of Mind: Classical and Contemporary Readings.* David J. Chalmers (ed.). New York: Oxford University Press, 219–26.

Nagel, T. (1989). *The View from Nowhere*. Oxford University Press.

Nietzsche, F. (1988). *On the Genealogy of Morality*. Maudemarie Clark and Alan J. Swensen (trans.). Indianapolis: Hackett Publishing Company, Inc.

Pine, F. (1990). *Drive, Ego, Object, and Self.* New York: Basic Books.

Putnam, H. (1988). *The Many Faces of Realism*. Chicago: Open Court Publishing Company.

Quine, W. V. O. & Ullian, J. S. *Web of Belief, 2nd Ed.* New York: Random House

Scheffler, I. (1982). *Science and Subjectivity, 2nd Ed.* Indianapolis: Hackett Publishing Company.

Sulloway, F. (1992). *Freud, Biologist of the Mind: Beyond the Psychoanalytic Legend.* Cambridge, MA: Harvard University Press.

Tauber, A. I. (2010). *Freud: The Reluctant Philosopher.* Princeton University Press.

Van Fraasen, B. (1980). *The Scientific Image.* Oxford: Clarendon Press

Van Fraasen, B. (2010). *Scientific Representation.* Oxford: Oxford University Press.

Index

About the Authors

M. Andrew Holowchak is a professional philosopher and historian, who teaches philosophy at University of Colorado, Colorado Springs. He has published voluminously on subjects such as ethics, psychoanalysis, Thomas Jefferson, ancient philosophy and science, philosophy of sport, and social and political philosophy and has authored/edited over thirty-five peer-reviewed books, He is author/editor of four books on Sigmund Freud: *Was the Death Drive the Death Knell of Freudian Psychoanalysis? Sigmund Freud on Repetition, Compulsion to Repeat, and the Death Drive*, with Michael Lavin, Lexington, 2018; *Freud: From Individual Psychology to Group Psychology,* Jason Aronson Press, 2012; *Radical Essays on Freudian Psychoanalysis: Point/Counterpoint*, Jason Aronson Press, 2012; and *Freud and Utopia: From Cosmological Narcissism to the "Soft Dictatorship" of Reason,* Lexington Books, 2011. He is also editor of the Thomas Jefferson Heritage Society's journal, *Journal of Thomas Jefferson's Life and Times.*

Michael Lavin is a Department of Army psychologist. He has worked in a variety of settings as a psychologist, including private practice. He holds a PhD in psychology from the University of Arizona. He also hold a PhD in Philosophy and Humanities from Stanford, and worked for a number of years at the University of Tennessee before resigning from his tenured associate professorship to retrain as a psychologist. He has done postdoctoral work at the University of Wisconsin Medical School and at the University of Minnesota's Program in Human Sexuality. He also studied psychoanalysis at the Baltimore-Washington Institute of Psychoanalysis and Short-term Intensive Psychodynamic Therapy at the Washington School of Psychiatry. He writes on topics related to psychology and ethics.

www.ingramcontent.com/pod-product-compliance
Ingram Content Group UK Ltd.
Pitfield, Milton Keynes, MK11 3LW, UK
UKHW041123071026
15587UKWH00009B/108